# VAJRAYĀNA
# BUDDHIST CENTRES IN SOUTH INDIA

# VAJRAYĀNA BUDDHIST CENTRES IN SOUTH INDIA

B. SUBRAHMANYAM

BKP

BHARATIYA KALA PRAKASHAN
DELHI (INDIA)

First Published : 2001



*Published by*
**C.P. Gautam**
BHARATIYA KALA PRAKASHAN
3421-A, IInd Floor, Narang Colony, Tri Nagar,
Delhi-110035. Phone : 7153083

**ISBN : 81-86050-59-0**

*Laser Type Setting by*
A-ONE GRAPHICS
X-4, Gali-2, Brahmapuri, Delhi-110053
Phone : 218 3470

*Printed at*
Santosh Offset Press
Inderlok, Delhi

**Dedicated To**

**ANANDA BUDDHA VIHARA TRUST**
Mahendra Hills
Secunderabad-500 026.
Telephone : (040)-7732421
Fax : (040) 7733160
Email : iananda@yahoo.com

# CONTENTS


| | | |
|---|---|---|
| | FOREWORD | *(ix)* |
| | PREFACE | *(xi)* |
| | ABBREVIATIONS | *(xv)* |
| | LIST OF PLATES | *(xvii)* |
| **1.** | **INTRODUCTION** | **1-11** |
| **2.** | **VAJRAYĀNA BUDDHIST CENTRES** | **12-98** |
| | Andhra Pradesh | 13 |
| | Tamilnadu | 70 |
| | Pondicherry | 82 |
| | Karnataka | 87 |
| | Kerala | 97 |
| **3.** | **CONCLUSION** | **99-104** |
| | **BIBLIOGRAPHY** | **105-110** |
| | **INDEX** | **111-116** |

# FOREWORD

Dr. B. Subrahmanyam, by virtue of his position as an Archaeological Officer in the State Department of the Archaeology & Museums, Hyderabad, being closely associated with explorations, excavations, conservation of excavated Buddhist sites and monuments, transplantation of temples and publication of reports, has aptly selected the study of one of the untouched areas of Buddhism i.e. *"Vajrayāna Buddhist Centres in South India"*. He deserves to be congratulated for taking up a herculean task not only collecting the published and unpublished data, but also for identifing a variety of icons and images discovered from different regions of south India and correlate with the relevant *dhyānas* and *sādhanas* mentioned in the Taṅtric texts such as *Guhya samaja taṅtra, Advayavajra Saṅgraha, Niṣpannayōgavaḷi, Sādhanamāla* etc.

The book encapsules the entire cultural data of the Vajrayāna phase from different states of south India and examines besides the causes for the rise and development of Vajrayāna Buddhist tradition comprehensively.

The important aspects dealtwith in the present work are the rise and development of *Śakti* and the *Pañcha Vīra* cult both in Brahmanical and Buddhist pantheons. He has given logical interpretations in the light of available evidences and presented conclusions very convincingly. He also showed various reasons, for the transformation of the pre-Buddhist cult of *Lajjagauri* or Nude Mother Goddess and as to how it conceives the form of Harītī in Buddhist pantheon. He has also explained as to how She became the tutelary Goddess for the Chālukyas, Kadaṁbas and Rāṣṭrakūṭas, who were basically Saivites. The book will not only be useful as of a reference book but also serves as a source material for the students working on Vajrayāna Buddhism in South India.

I congratulate Dr. B. Subrahmanyam for his commendable work on the Vajrayāna Buddhism. I hope this work will draw the attention of the scholars and students and will definitely generate interest among the researchers to carry out further studies in this field.

Hyderabad
27.08.2000

—**Dr. V.V. Krishna Sastry**
(EX-DIRECTOR)
*DEPT.* ARCHAEOLOGY & MUSEUMS
HYDERABAD, A.P.

# PREFACE

Unlike the other religions of India, Buddhism never confined itself to the limits of India but travelled smoothly and silently across the world, disseminating its eccentricitic ideas from time to time, more particularly, in the Taṅtric age (4th-5th c. A.D.). This age witnessed not only the gradual decline of Buddhism, but also saw the resurgence of Vedic Brahmanism. To withstand the on slaught of neo-Brahmanis, the Buddhists had no option but to seek the help of Tantricists, probably to induct Taṅtricism into the orthodox Buddhism and in order make the religion more populate and attractive. Candidly speaking, it was a remarkable transformation in the history of Buddhism when it passed on to the stage of theism from aetheism.

To understand this transistional stage within the parameters of the religion, it is necessary to study the material culture of the Taṅtric age such as stone images, metal icons of *Dhyāni* Buddhas, Bōddhisattvas, various Gods and Goddesses and stone and terracotta plaques engraved with Buddhist creed formulae.

In the early phase of Buddhism (*Thēravāda*), the Buddha was merely portrayed for worship in the form of a *Stūpa,* Footprints, Throne, Bodhi tree, Pillar of fire, besides various episodes contained the *Jataka* stories and the great events in the life of Buddha which quite often found in the schools of Sanchi, Barhut, Amaravati and Gandhara. In the Mahāyāna phase of Buddhism, idol worship became a prominent feature. According to Foucher, the practice of treating the image of Buddha as *Lokottara* or *Bhagavan* was initiated and modelled by the sculptor of Gandhara School of Art and later on perfection attained in the hands of the artists of Amaravati and Mathura Schools.

Efforts of erudite scholars like Waddell, Grunwedel, Foucher, Burgess, Getty etc. in the field of Buddhist archaeology resulted in unravelling the several unknown features of Mahāyana phase of Buddhism to the Buddhist world, particularly about the last phase i.e. Taṅtrayāna or Vajrayāna. The publication of two great works on 'Etudes Sur I' Iconography Bouddhique de L'Inde' by Prof, Foucher, in the years 1900 and 1905 literally inspired the Indian scholars like B. Hara Prasad Sastri, B. Bhattacharya, A.K. Coomara Swamy, N.K. Bhattasali, D.C. Bhattacharya etc. to work on this rich untouched field of research.

Afterwards, several scholars in India and abroad took keen interest in the subject and definitely substantial work has been turned out specially on various aspects of the early phase of Buddhism. Truly speaking, inadequate attention was paid to the Taṅtric aspects of Buddhism, obviously because of the paucity of texts in Sanskrit literature, to identify several taṅtric images and icons at Saranath, Nalanda, Kurkhihar, Vikramaśilā and several other sites in eastern India. With the publication of several manuscripts such as *Guḥya Samāja Taṅtra, Sādhana Māla, Niṣpanna-yōgāvali, Advaya Vajra Saṅgraḥa* and many more works made it easy for the scholars to identifying the various Taṅtric images and icons with their relevant *sādhanas* or *dhyānas*. Basing on the occurrence of several Taṅtric images from eastern India, it appears that the Vajrayāna or Taṅtrayāna had its roots only in eastern Indian states, particularly Bengal, Bihar and Orrisa, and from here it spread to the other parts of the sub-continent.

As we know, Buddhism though it had its origin in northern India, it flourished only upto early medieval times, whereas in south India, it enjoyed right from its beginning and survived as one of the major religions upto the late medieval times i.e. post-Vijayanagara times (17th century A.D.). The occurrence of innumerable sites (3rd c. B.C. to 15th-16th c. A.D.) on hill tops, near coastal strips, river valleys and fertile river banks obviously suggests that early Buddhism had a long span in South India. Here, it was nurtured and flourished under royal patronage and transformed into the vibrant Mahāyāna tradition and later on passed on to the Taṅtrayāna or Vajrayāna.

In South India, the Vajrayāna—the last phase of Buddhism has left ineffable mark by way of producing innumerable early Taṅtric images and icons. The study is itself a fascinating and alluring subject which lends great leeway for understanding the flourishing conditions of Vajrayāna Buddhism in South India.

On this far-reaching subject, except for fragmentary information in the form of small articles in various journals, no comprehensive study has so far been made. Earlier some attempts have been made by several scholars. Dr. K. Krishna Murthy studied a few Vajrayāna sculptrures from Amaravati and Salihundam in Andhra Pradesh, while Dr. S. Nagaraju worked on the Vestiges of Buddhist Art in Karnataka. Dr. A. Aiyyappan and P.R. Srinivasan studied the sculptures of Tamil Nadu and Kerala while T.N. Ramachandran on the Bronzes of South India. These scholars have studied the above discoveries in isolation and furnished only the descriptive accounts of the stone images and Bronze icons, with little attention to the origin and evolution of Gods and Goddesses, their *sādhanas* and *dhyānas,* their bearing on to the textual descriptions and comparative studies and so on.

The discovery of some early bronze icons such as Harītī (1st-2nd c. A. D.) from Dhulikatta, Avalokiteśwara from Nelakondapalli (4th-5th c. A.D.) in A.P. and other Vajrayāna images from various parts of South India, particularly more from Andhra Pradesh, literally inspired me to take up this work in a wider perspective incorporating all available materials. The discovery of simple and small icons and images coupled with literary evidences suggests the beginnings of Vajrayāna cult in South India in general and Andhra Pradesh in particular. From here, the Vajrayāna cult might have spread to the other parts of India and abroad through coastal routes. I hope that this work will not only serve the specialists in the subject, but also will be useful to the students, artists, connoisseurs and researchers, who have been attracted by the rich spiritual and cultural heritage of Buddhism and Buddhist art.

For the publication of this work, many scholars and intellectuals came forward and extended their help to whom I owe a deep debut of gratitude.

I take this opportunity to thank Sri V. Sarma Rao, IAS, Dr. Lal Rosem, IAS and Sri A. Ramalakshman, IAS who served as Commissioners of Archaeology & Museums Department, Hyderabad for permitting me to make use of the departmental materials in the present book.

I have also received immense help and scholarly advice from Sri C. Anjaneya Reddy, IPS, Sri S. Veeranarayana Reddy, IPS and Dr. K.C.P. Gandhi. They are always in the process of disseminating right thoughts and moral teachings based on the Buddha *Dharma* to the people who assemble in the Temple Complex of Ananda Buddha Vihara, Mahendra Hills, Secunderabad, and thus serving for the upliftment of Buddhist culture in Andhra Pradesh. In fact they are primarily responsible for my working on various untouched aspects of Buddhist archaeology in Andhra Pradesh. At the same time, I also express my gratitude to the members of Ananda Buddha Vihara Trust for extending their valuable co-operation and help particularly in allowing me to utilize reference books available in the Temple Library.

I will be failing in my duty if I do not acknowledge the scholarly support and suggestions received from the eminent scholars like Dr. V.V. Krishna Sastry, Dr.I.K. Sarma, Prof. Radhakrishna Sarma and Dr. A.K.V.S. Reddy, Director, Salarjung Museum, Hyderabad, and also other officers like Dr. P.R. Murthy (Retd), Dr. N.S. Ramachandra Murthy, Dy. Director (Epigraphy) and Sri. P. Jogi Naidu, Dy. Director (Museums) State Archaeological department, Hyderabad.

I also extend my thanks to the authorities of the Archaeological Survey of India and Commisioner of Archaeology & Museums, A.P., Hyderabad for permitting me to utilize their photographs, sketches and drawings of the respective departments.

My thanks are also due to Sri P. Vengala Reddy, Asst. Director, Sri P.V.

Sarma, Asst. Director, Dr. E. Sivanagi Reddy, Draughtsman, Dr. K. Padmanabha, Dr. Suguna Sarma, Dr. Brahmachari, Sri D. Pattabhi Reddy, Sri G. Venkataratnam and Sri D. Prakash Technical Assistants Department of Archaeology & Museums for their constant help in arranging the chapters and offering valuable suggestions. I am also thankful to Sri J.V. Sainath and Sri G. Narasimha Rao, Photographers for supplying good photographs.

I also take opportunity to thank Smt. B. Indumathi Devi, Smt. R. Anjanamani and Smt. U. Laxmi Devi, Technical Assistants (Publication) for carrying out proof corrections with great care.

My sincere thanks are also due to Sri Md. Mustafa, Special Category Steno and Smt. R.V. Devika Rani, Typist, for typing the manuscript with great care and diligence.

In the end, I express my gratitude to Smt. G. Varalakshmi, Librarian (Gazetted) for her help in lending library facilities and I also record my thanks to Sri C.P. Gautam, M/s. Bharatiya Kala Prakashan, Delhi, for undertaking neat printing of the publication within a short time.

Hyderabad
Date : 27.08.2000

**Dr. B. Subrahmanyam**
Asst. Director (Excavations),
Dept. of Archaeology and
Museums, Govt. of A.P.,
Gunfoundry, Hyderabad-1.

# ABBREVIATIONS

| | |
|---|---|
| AAR | Annual Administrative Report, Department of Archaeology & Museums, Hyderabad, A.P. |
| AI | Ancient India—Bulletin of Archaeological Survey of India. |
| APJA | The Andhra Pradesh Journal of Archaeology. |
| ARAD | Annual Report of the Archaeological Department, ASI, Southern Circle. |
| ARADN | Annual Report of the Archaeological Department of H.E.H. the Nizam's Dominions. |
| ARASI | Annual Report of the Archaeological Survey of India, Southern circle, Madras. |
| ARIE | Annual Report on Indian Epigraphy. |
| ARSIE | Annual Report on South Indian Epigraphy. |
| ASI | Archaeological Survey of India, New Delhi. |
| BACRI | Birla Archaeological & Cultural Research Institute, Hyderabad. |
| EI | Epigraphia Indica. |
| EC | Epigraphia Carnataka. |
| IA | Indian Antiquary. |
| IAR | Indian Archaeology—A Review. |
| IHQ | Indian Historical Quarterly. |
| JAHRS | Journal of Andhra Historical Research Society. |
| JBORS | Journal of Bihar and Orissa Research Society. |
| JBRRAS | Journal of Bombay Research Royal Asiatic Society. |
| JESI | Journal of the Epigraphical Society of India. |
| JIH | Journal of Indian History. |
| JOI | Journal of Oriental Institute. |
| JRAS | Journal of Royal Asiatic Socity of Great Britain. |
| MASI | Memoirs of Archaeological Survey of India. |
| MSI | Mythic Society of India. |
| QJMS | Quarterly Journal of the Mythic Society. |
| QRHS | Quarterly Research in Historical Studies. |
| RSRC | Rayaprolu Subrahmanyam Memorial Research Centre, Guntur. |
| SVUOJ | Sri Venkateswara University Oriental Research Institute Journal. |

## LIST OF PLATES

Pl. 1. (c) Heruka, Gopalapatnam, Visakhapatnam District.
Pl. 2. Avalōkiteśvara, Ramatirtham, Prakasam Dist.
Pl. 3. Inscribed clay tabalets with *Dhāranis,* Sankaram, Visakhapatnam Dist.
Pl. 4. Buddha (Amitābha), Sankaram, Visakhapatnam Dist.
Pl. 5. Harītī, Sankaram, Visakhapatnam Dist.
Pl. 6. Bronze Icon of Harītī, Dhulikatta, Visakhapatnam Dist.
Pl. 7. Harītī, Karkaipalle, Visakhapatnam Dist.
Pl. 8. Taṅtric Image of Gaṇapati, Sankaram, Visakhapatnam Dist.
Pl. 9. Harītī, Nagarjunakonda, Guntur Dist.
Pl. 10. Bronze Icons of Buddha, Amaravati, Guntur Dist.
Pl. 11. Bronze Icons of Avalōkiteśvara, Amaravati, Guntur Dist.
Pl. 12. Buddha (Akṣobhya), Amaravati, Guntur Dist.
Pl. 13. Maitrēya, Amaravati, Guntur Dist.
Pl. 14. Buddha and Padmapāni, Amaravati, Guntur Dist.
Pl. 15 (a) Heruka, Amaravati, Guntur Dist.
Pl. 16. Sugati Sandarśanalōkēśvara, Amaravati, Guntur Dist.
Pl. 17. Khadiravaṇī Tārā, Amaravati, Guntur Dist.
Pl. 17 (a) Syāma Tārā, Amaravati, Guntur Dist.
Pl. 18. Heruka, Ugra Tārā & Maitreya, Amaravati, Guntur Dist.
Pl. 19. Jambhāla (stucco), Amaravati, Guntur Dist.
Pl. 20. Buddha flanked by Maitrēya and Padmapāṇi, Amaravati, Guntur Dist.
Pl. 21. Padmapāṇi, (British Museum, London), Amaravati, Guntur Dist.
Pl. 21 (a) Padmapāṇi, (British Museum, London), Amaravati, Guntur Dist.
Pl. 22. Avalōkiteśvara (British Museum, London), Amaravati, Guntur Dist.
Pl. 23. Buddha (Akṣobhya) (Madras Museum), Amaravati, Guntur Dist.
Pl. 24. Siṁhanāda Avalōkiteśvara, (Madras Museum), Amaravati, Guntur Dist.
Pl. 25. Mañjughōsha (Madras Museum), Amaravati, Guntur Dist.
Pl. 26. Buddha (Stucco), Salihundam, Srikakulam Dist.

Pl. 27. Mārīcī, Salihundam, Srikakulam Dist.

Pl. 27 (a) Back view (Mārīcī), Salihundam, Srikakulam Dist.

Pl. 28. Mārīcī, Salihundam, Srikakulam Dist.

Pl. 29. Vāgīśvara, Salihundam, Srikakulam Dist.

Pl. 30. Khasarpaṇa, Salihundam, Srikakulam Dist.

Pl. 31. Tārā, Salihundam, Srikakulam Dist.

Pl. 32. Sita Tārā, Salihundam, Srikakulam Dist.

Pl. 33. Maitreya, Salihundam, Srikakulam Dist.

Pl. 34. Padmapāṇi, Salihundam, Srikakulam Dist.

Pl. 35. Buddha (Akṣobhya), Salihundam, Srikakulam Dist.

Pl. 36. Buddha (Akṣobhya), Salihundam, Srikakulam Dist.

Pl. 37. Mañjusri, Salihundam, Srikakulam Dist.

Pl. 38. Bronze Icon of Padmapāṇi, Guntupalli, West Godavari Dist.

Pl. 39. Avalōkitēśvara, Gummadidurru, Krishna Dist.

Pl. 40 Buddha (Amitābha), Kunthuru, Nellore Dist.

Pl. 41. Buddha (Akṣobhya) Mukhalingam, Srikakulam Dist.

Pl. 42. Buddha (Amitābha) Mukhalingam, Srikakulam Dist.

Pl. 43. Uṣṇiṣa Vijaya, Mukhalingam, Srikakulam Dist.

Pl. 44. Harītī, Takkallapadu, Krishna Dist.

Pl. 45. Buddha (Amitābha), Kollapattu, Nellore Dist.

Pl. 46. Buddha (Akṣobhya), Vaikunthapuram, Guntur Dist.

Pl. 47. Padmapāni, Nandayapalem, Guntur Dist.

Pl. 48. Bronze Icons of Buddha as Padmapāṇi, Buddham, Guntur Dist.

Pl. 49. Bronze Icon of Avalōkitēśvara (Front and Back views), Nelakondapalli, Khammam Dist.

Pl. 50 (a) Head of Avalōkitēśvara showing silver inlaid eyes and *urṇa,* Nelakondapalli, Khammam Dist.

Pl. 50 (b) Close up view of Avalōkitēśvara, Nelakondapalli, Khammam Dist.

Pl. 51. Maitrēya, Melaiyur, Tanjore Dist.

Pl. 52. Buddha in dhyāna mudrā, Tyagnur, Salem Dist.

Pl. 52 (a) Buddha in dhyāna mudrā, Tyagnur, Salem Dist.

Pl. 53. Buddha (Amitābha), Elaiyur, Tanjore Dist.

Pl. 54. Buddha (Amitābha), Manambady, Tanjore Dist.

Pl. 54 (a) Bronze icon of standing Buddha with flaming *uṣṇīṣa,* Tanjore, Tanjore Dist.

Pl. 55. Buddha (Amitābha), Tanjore, Tanjore Dist.
Pl. 56. Buddha (Amitābha), Tiruvatti, South Arcot Dist.
Pl. 57 (a) Buddha (Amitābha), Jayanakonda Cholapuram, Tiruchirapalli Dist.
Pl. 57 (b) Buddha (Amitābha), Jayanakonda Cholapuram, Tiruchirapalli Dist.
Pl. 57 (c) Buddha (Amitābha), Jayanakonda Cholapuram, Tiruchirapalli Dist.
Pl. 58. Buddha (Akṣobhya), Kanchipuram.
Pl. 59. Buddha (Amitābha), Kanchipuram.
Pl. 60 (a) Buddha, Kanchipuram.
Pl. 60 (b) Buddha, Kanchipuram.
Pl. 60 (c) Buddha, Kanchipuram.
Pl. 61. Bronze Icon of Buddha with flaming *uṣṇīṣa,* Nagapattanam.
Pl. 61 (a) Buddha (Akṣobhya), Nagapattanam.
Pl. 62. Buddha in *vyakhyana mudrā (Bronze),* (Fine Arts Museum, Boston), Nagapattanam.
Pl. 63. Buddha (Akṣobhya), Nagapattanam.
Pl. 63 (a) Buddha in *dhyāna mudrā* (11th c. A.D., Norton Simon Museum of Arts, Pasadena), Nagapattanam.
Pl. 63 (b) Head of a Buddha with flaming *uṣṇīṣa* (11th c. A.D.) (Art Institute of Chicago), Nagapattanam.
Pl. 63 (c) Amitābha (9th c. A.D.) (The Brooklyn Museum), Nagapattanam.
Pl. 64. Buddha (Amitābha) Bronze, Nagapattanam.
Pl. 65. Avalōkitēśvara, Nagapattanam.
Pl. 65 (a) Avalōkitēśvara (17th A.D.), Bronze, Nagapattanam.
Pl. 66. Maitrēya (Bronze, Front & Back views), Nagapattanam.
Pl. 67. Maitrēya (Bronze), Nagapattanam.
Pl. 67 (a) Maitrēya (17th A.D. Bronze), Nagapattanam.
Pl. 68. Ṣaḍakṣari Lōkēśvara (Bronze), Nagapattanam.
Pl. 69. Padmapāṇi (Bronze), Nagapattanam.
Pl. 70. Khadiravāṇi Tārā (Bronze), Nagapattanam.
Pl. 70 (a) Tārā (Bronze), Nagapattanam.
Pl. 71. Lōkēśvara (Bronze), Nagapattanam.
Pl. 72. Jambhala (Bronze), Nagapattanam.
Pl. 73. Jaṁbhala and Vasudhara, Nagapattanam.
Pl. 74. Buddha (Amitābha), Manikandi, Ramanathapuram Dist.
Pl. 75. Buddha (Amitābha), Kuvam, Chengalput Dist.

Pl. 76. Buddha (Amitābha), Arikamedu, Pondicherry.
Pl. 77. Buddha (Amitābha), Karadikuppam, Pondicherry.
Pl. 78. Buddha in *vyakhyana mudrā* (Bronze), Kadri, Mangalore.
Pl. 79. Lōkanātha (Bronze), Kadri, Mangalore.
Pl. 80. Hālāhala Lōkēśvara (Bronze), Kadri, Mangalore.
Pl. 81. Close up view, Hālāhala, showing inlaid silver eyes and *urṇa,* Kadri, Mangalore.
Pl. 82. Tārā-Bhagavati, Belagami, Shimoga Dist.

# AREA OF STUDY

## Important Vajrayāna Buddhist Centres in South India

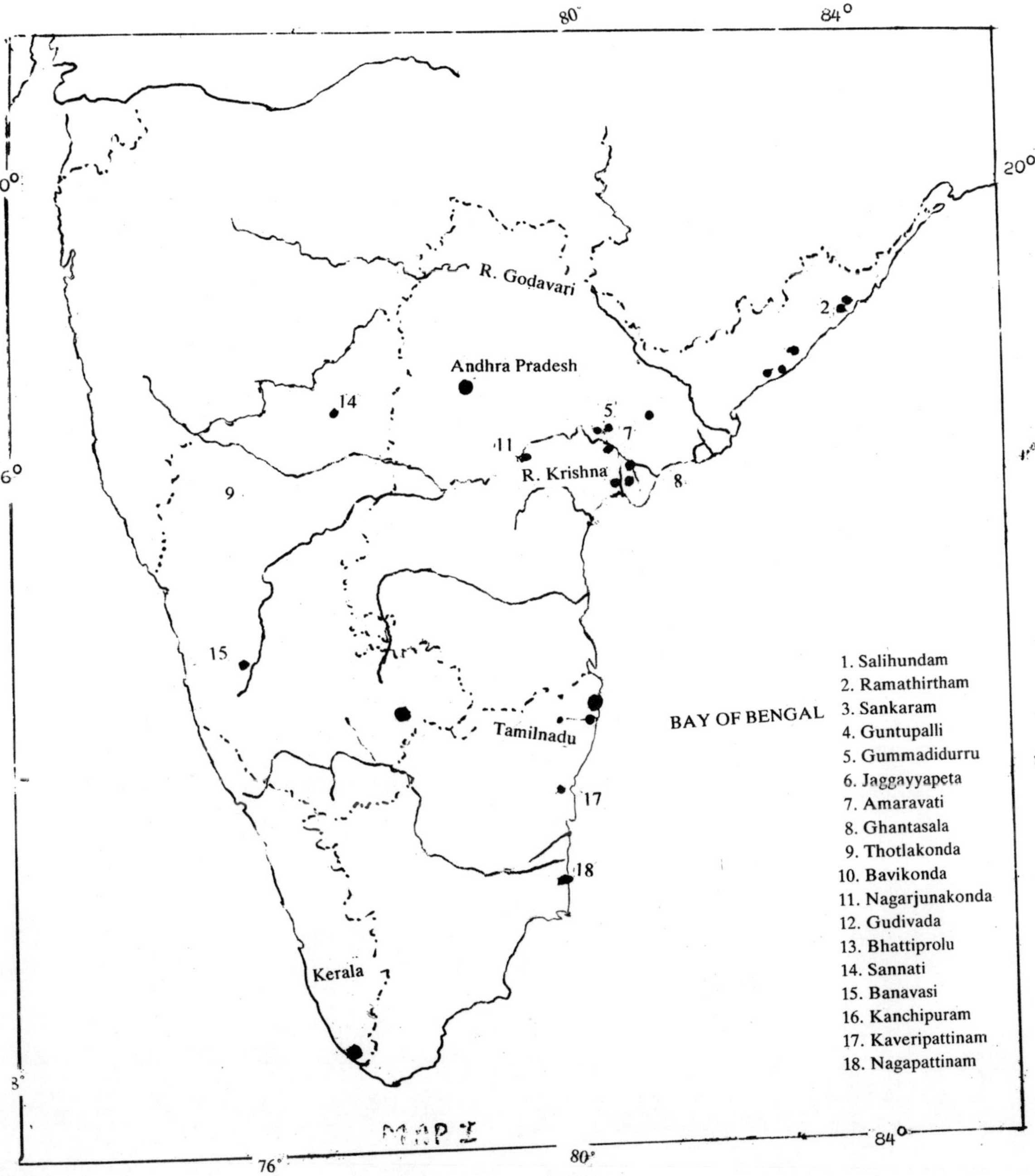

# INTRODUCTION

Vajrayāna, otherwise known as Taṅtrayāna or Maṅtrayāna is an offshoot of Mahāyāna, literally based on the *Mādhyamika* (*Śūnyavāda*) or *Bōdhisattvayāna* school of philosophy, consolidated by Āchārya Nagarjuna.[1] The term Vajrayāna though literally means adamantine or the Thunderbolt vehicle, in Buddhist philosophy it applies to *Śūnya* which symbolically represented by *Vajra* (Thunderbolt). The Vajrayanists believe that *Śūnya* stand for ultimate reality and hence the innumerable gods and goddesses are *Śūnya* in essence. In this doctrine, when the Bodhi mind attains *Nirvāṇa*, it merges in *Śūnya* and there it remains in eternal bliss and happiness. In Vajrayāna, *Nirvāṇa* comprised three elements viz., *Śūnya*, *Vijñāna* and *Mahāsukha*. The commingling of the three is termed as *Vajra* which is firm and that can not be cut, changed, burnt, destroyed, pierced or penetrated but which destroys all evils. Hence, the Buddha was represented as the Supreme (*Ādi*) Buddha Vajrasattva or Vajradhara, a holder of the Thunderbolt. The weapon *Vajra* or Thunderbolt is shown in Buddhist sculptures as a staff with five prongs which symbolically represent the five divine forms of *Dhyāni* Buddhas (*Pañcha Buddhas*). *Vajra* is also the name of a weapon usually held by ascetics and monks. Vajrayāna teaches a monistic (Advaita) philosophy in which all beings are *Vajra-sattvas* and only one that Vajrasattva is immanent in all beings.[2]

In order to understand the origin and development of Vajrayāna philosophy it is necessary to study the early tenets of the Buddhist *Saṅgha*. In the beginning, there were two *yānas* (vehicles) in the *Saṅgha viz. Śravakayāna* and *Pratyēka Buddhayāna*.[3] The *Śravakas* were to hear from a Buddha and preach. They could neither attain *Nirvāṇa* by themselves nor help others attain it, whereas the *Pratyēkas* were eminent persons, who could attain *Nirvāṇa* by their own efforts, without the help of a Buddha but they could not impart *Nirvāṇa* to others. Both these *yānas* were explained logically in the philosophical theories of *Vaibhāṣika* (*Vāhyārthabhaṅga*). With the advent of Mahāyāna or *Bōdhisattvayāna*, the earlier *yānas* were over shadowed. The Mādhyamikas or Mahāyanists claimed that they could attain *Nirvāṇa* and Buddhahood with their unaided efforts and could help others attain these ideals. The Mahāyāna was further sub-classified into *Pāramitayāna* and *Maṅtrayāna*. The former was expounded by the philosophical schools of

*Sautrāntika* (*Sarvaṣṭivāda*), *Śūnyavāda* (*Mādhyamikavāda*) and *Yōgacāra* (*Vijñānavāda*) while the latter, by the philosophical schools of *Yōgacāra* and *Śūnyavāda*. The Vajrayāna or *Taṅtrayāna* came as Yōgacāra school of philosophy inspired by *Śūnyavāda* of the Mādhyamikas, with an element of *Vijñāna*.[4] It was probably propounded during the time of Asanga (3rd c. A.D.)[5]

According to the Vijñānavādins, the process of Liberation or *Nirvāṇa* contains two elements i.e. *Śūnya* and *Vijñāna*. In the philosophy of Vijñānavādins, the mind of a Bodhi undergoes frequent changes from preceding moments to succeeding ones with the same memory, conformations and qualities and this cycle goes on till the *Vijñāna* attains liberation. In the *Yōgacāra* and *Vijñāna* schools of philosophy, when emancipation was obtained, it no longer remains *Śūnya* but turns into eternal consciousness whereas in the Vajrayāna the path led to perfect enlightenment (*Anuttārā Saṁyak Saṁbōdhi*).

Probably, even during the life time of the Buddha, the ideological concepts of the preachers varied. Every preacher tried to refine the existing magical practices in order to attract and bring more people under his fold. It appears that the organisers allowed some of the magical practices into their new religion to make it more attractive and popular. It is often asked whether the *Taṅtras* were ever taught by the Buddha or existed during the life time of the Buddha. The early Buddhist tradition says that it was common for the Buddha to deliver in all kinds of unusual circumstances. On some occasions he taught in response to the request of a God or Super-human being, even the *Abhidharma* which is believed to have been taught to his mother in the Heaven of the Thirty-three. It is generally believed that the Mahāyāna masters receive instructions through extraordinary means. The Vajrayanists believe that texts of Mind only school were taught to Asanga by the future Buddha Maitrēya. By this way the taṅtras said to have been transmitted from one to the other. If the Buddha did not teach the *taṅtras* at once to every one surely it was because that not every one was able to appreciate and understand their true significance.[6]

Though, it is a fact that the Buddha was antagonistic to all sorts of sacrifices, sorcery, necromancy or magic, yet circumstances might have compelled him to allow the members of the *Saṅgha* to practice primitive or non-rigid formulae such as *Mudrās, Maṇḍalas, Yōga* and *Taṅtras*. It is also possible that after the *Mahāparinirvāṇa*, some of the sects or *Saṅghas* allowed the members to practise Tāṅtricism in order to make *Nirvāṇa* easy and also to make the religion popular. Otherwise, the abrupt or sudden advent of *Taṅtrayāna* or *Maṅtrayāna* into the orthodox Buddhism cannot be explained logically.

Tāṅtricism explains the various means of attaining *Nirvāṇa* easily, by linking a series of magical spells to the meditational techniques and rituals. By practising *Dharaṇis, Maṇḍalas* and *Mudrās*, the initiate meditates on one or the other aspect of the Buddha and thus achieve Union with him. By this, the essence of the Mahāyāna teachings i.e. the role of Bōdhisattva was by-passed.[7] The *Maṅtras*, comprising mystic symbols embody a few intelligible words which are shorter than the *Dharaṇis*. By muttering these *Maṅtras*, one could easily attain Salvation. The *Maṅtra*, therefore, means something that protects the mind. It also means in general the esoteric or secret vehicle, whereas the *Taṅtra* means the extension or continuity of knowledge just like a thread in the fabric. Generally, a *Maṅtra* recounts the names of the divinity or his attributes. *Maṅtra Śāstra* prescribes ways for a person to obtain attainment. By doing this, the senses of the person are sharpened to the highest degree, for the *Maṅtras* are endowed with divine power due to the arrangement of the syllables. These constitute the backbone of the Vajrayāna worship. *Advaya Vajra,* author of *Tattva Ratnāvali* (12th century A.D.) comments that *Maṅtra Śāstra* transcends all other *Śāstras*.[8]

The *Śūnyavāda* or *Mādhyamika* school of philosophy postulates the theory of transcendental state. To the *Mādhyamikas*, the subject is either in existence or non-existence or a combination or negation of the two. For them, both the subject and object are *Śūnya* in essence and there is no reality (void) either of the mind or the eternal world. In this doctrine, a new element *viz. Mahāsukha* (eternal bliss) was introduced by the *Yōgacāra* school of philosophy into its concept of liberation. Scholars are of the opinion that the doctrine of Vajrayāna emanated from the concept of *Mahāsukha.*[9] *Advaya vajra* also accepts the theory of *Mahāsukha* and explains logically about attaining *Nirvāṇa* without the *Śakti,* the embodiment of *Karuṇa* (compassion).

The reasons for the introduction of the Vajrayāna school of philosophy into orthodox Buddhism seem to be the gradual slackening of disciplinary regulations in the *Saṅgha* and also the growing popularity of magical rites among the masses for attaining salvation easily.

The other causes for the rise of Vajrayāna school were the existence of three thought currents that were prevalent in Buddha's life time *viz.* (a) the democratic (b) the magical or ritual and (c) the symbolic current. The democratic current practices the highest fruits of religious life i.e. attaining enlightenment by the laity. A classic example comes from the Buddhist tradition i.e. the attainment of *Arhatship* by the Buddha's father Suddhodana while still he was a layman. Examples of magical or ritual current are found in the accounts of Pali canon. The Buddha pronouncing formulae of protection against snake bite and the perils of child birth, conversion of the queen Kṣēma, rituals like the removal of the hair and donning of yellow robes etc. and the process of conversion of Kṣēma in which the Buddha creates the vision of various stages of decay of life in a matter of moments. Here, Buddha used supernatural powers to create an apparition that would teach the truth of impermanence.

In the symbolic current, symbols were used to explain the events in the life of Buddha. For example, the wheel was used to indicate the *Dharma* and the symbol of lute to suggest the middle path. In the early Buddhist tradition, the above three currents of thought and action i.e. the democratic, magic or ritual and symbolic, were the main elements that contributed to the growth of Vajrayāna tradition.[10]

The Vajrayāna school of philosophy exhorted easy methods such as chanting the *Dharaṇis, Mantras*, panegyrics and worship of gods and goddesses to attain salvation. Though some of these principles were webbed indirectly into the main-stream of Buddhism, it was only after gaining popularity, the tenets, rites and practices were preached and practised publicly. The new doctrine satisfied every individual of the lower and higher ranks of the society, the pious as well as the sinners.

According to the early tenets of Buddhism, Buddha never believed in the existence of God or worship. In support of the above theory may be cited a classic example found in *Saundarānanda* of Aśvaghōṣa, in which Buddha discouraged his half-brother Nanda who tried to touch his feet in token of reverence and instead he advised him to follow the precepts of *Saddharma*. This shows that Buddha was antagonistic to the worship of God or even a great person.[11]

Evidence for worship of God in the early school of Buddhism (*Thēravāda* or Hinayāna) (4th-3rd c. B.C.) is conspicuously absent. However, to the Buddhists of this school, the most sacred object was the *stūpa* or *chaitya* besides other objects of symbolic worship. For example, in the early art of Sāñchi, Amaravati and Barhut, Buddha images are conspicuous by their absence whereas in Mahāyāna Buddhism (1st-2nd c. A.D), Buddha was defied and considered as super-human or *Lōkōttārā*. With the result, a large number of deities emerged and even the three jewels of Buddhism came to be worshipped in the form of deities. It is believed that the first image of Buddha was carved at Gāndhāra by the Graceo-Buddhists and later on at Mathura. Afterwards, Vajrayāna Buddhism (from 5th-6th c. A.D. onwards) witnessed the emergence of various gods and goddesses.

The Vajrayāna philosophy believes that the Universe is composed of five cosmic elements or *Skandhas viz.* (1) *Rūpa* (form) (2) *Vēdana* (consciousness) (3) *Saṁjña* (name) (4) *Saṁskāra* (conformation) and (5) *Vijñāna* (consciousness). These elements are defined as five Dhyāni Buddhas *viz.* Vairocana, Akṣobhya, Ratnasambhava, Amitābha and Amōghasiddhi. These are considered as progenitors of the five *kulas* or families of gods and goddesses. It is for the first time in the *Guhyasamāja* are found the names of the five Dhyāni Buddhas, their names, families, *Mudrās*, *Maṅtras*, *Śaktis* or female counterparts, their colours and directions. The *Dhyāni* Buddhas are a peculiar class of Buddhas, who are eternal and do have not to pass through the lower stages of the Bōdhisattva.[12]

Generally, the Lord Vairocana, the central figure (Ādi Buddha) is represented in *Dharmachakra* or *Uttarabōdhi mudrā* whose primary affliction is ignorance.. He is shown in white colour. His *Vāhana* is a pair of dragons or gryhons. He is the Lord of Ether, whose sensory function is 'sound'. Amitābha, the lord of the water, positioned on the East is shown in red colour whose sensory function is taste and whose primary affliction is attachment. He is depicted as in meditation. His *Vāhana* is a pair of peacocks. Amōghasiddhi is the lord of North whose colour is green and his sensory function is smell. His *Vāhana* is a pair of *Garudas*. His representative element is Earth. He is shown in *abhaya mudrā*. Akṣōbhya is the lord of West and his representative element is Air. His colour is blue and the sensory function is touch. He is shown in *bhūmisparśa mudrā* whose primary affliction is ill-will. His *Vāhana* is a pair of elephants. On the South is the Lord Ratna Sambhava, shown in *Varada* attitude. His representative element is Fire. His *vāhana* is a pair of lions. His colour is yellow and the sensory function is sight.[13]

Mañjuśrī, another *Dhyāni* Buddha was added afterwards, to the group of the five *Dhyāni* Buddhas along with the other three, making altogether nine *Dhyāni* Buddhas. Here, in Vajrayāna the Buddha as a God is shown amidst women instead of pious Bōdhisattvas.

All the *Dhyāni* Buddhas are passive and deep in meditation. They take no part in the affairs of the world whereas their counterparts are the Bōdhisattvas who exert influence over the Universe in successive years through human beings (Mānushi Buddhas). The Bōdhisattvas are *Sāmantabhadra, Vajrapāṇi, Ratnapāṇi, Avalōkitēśwara and Viśvapāṇi* and their respective Mānushi Buddhas are *Krakuchanda, Kanakamuni, Kasyapa, Gautama and Maitrēya*. It was the *Dhyāni* Buddha concept that introduced the worship of *Prajñā* or *Śakti* in Buddhism. The emanations or offsprings of these *Dhyani* Buddhas are depicted with an effigy of parental *Dhyāni* Buddha on the crown or *taira*, suggesting from whom they emanated.

The main objective in this philosophy is the realisation of god. The Tāṅtricists, by their constant efforts through mental exercises, obtain supernatural powers called *Siddhis* and those who gained these *Siddhis* were called *Siddhas*. The process through which they obtained *Siddhi* was called *Sādhana* (practise). This doctrine required competent preceptors and efficient disciples (*Adhikārṇis*) who had patience and zeal to follow the prescribed practices. The disciples should be proficient in the art of *Yōga* and *Haṭhayōga,* without which, it would be difficult to practise Tāṅtricism and achieve visualization of the deity.[14]

The process of realisation or visualisation of the deity is important which is known as 'Means' (*upāya*). It has four elements such as *sēva, upasādhana, sādhana* and *maṅtrasādhana*. *Sēva* or worship is divided into ordinary (*sāmānya*) and excellent (*uttama*). The ordinary worship has four kinds of *Vajras* (1) the conception of *Śūnyata*, (2) its transformation into germ syllable, (3) its evolution in the form of a deity and (4) the representation of the deity, whereas the excellent worship has six processes *viz.* breath control (*pratyahara*), (2) meditation (*dhyāna*), (3) breath control (*prāṇayāma*), (4) memory (*anusmrti*), (5) meditation (*dhāraṇa*) and (6) visualisation (*samādhi*).[15]

In the realisation of the deity, three main elements are involved *viz.* the worshipper (*Bōdhicitta*), the deity (*Maṅtra Purusha or Maṅtra* body) and their connection or identity (*Ahamikara*). The deity is the embodiment of the cluster of letters or words contained in a *Maṅtra* and they are dynamized by concentration and by excessive repetition evoking strong vibrations and condense themselves into the form of deities which is known as the *Maṅtra Purusa* or *Maṅtra* body. Before visualising the deity or *Maṅtrapuruṣa*, a complete identity between *Bōdhicitta* (the worshipper) and the *Maṅtrapuruṣa* is necessary.[16]

In this doctrine, the worshipper should have desire or psychic force (*bhāvana*) to visualise the deity. This desire reacts on the infinite energy (*Śūnya*) which gives rise to the various manifestations, depending on the nature of reaction which is of unlimited variety and the resultant deity therefore is also seen in infinite variety of forms.

Thus, there is no real existence of God in Vajrayāna Buddhism. The deities have no prescribed form, which mainly depends on the mental visualisation of the *Sādhakas* and the method of worship. It is the moral responsibility of a *Sādhaka* to record the process by which the visualisation of a particular deity took place to enable the other disciples to follow.[17]

In Vajrayāna Buddhism, *Śūnyata* is identified with compassion which manifested itself in different forms to discharge different functions. For example, if any disease is to be cured, the *Śūnya* takes the form of *Siṁhanada*. Similarly, for snake bite—*Janguli*, for destruction—*Mahākāla*, for love affairs—*Kurukuḷḷa* etc. In this doctrine, the conception of the multitude of Buddhist deities emerges from one grand conception of *Śūnya*. Importance is given to the colour, weapons and *asanās* of gods. The gods are represented as carrying the *Bōdhicitta* (will to enlightenment) in their hands and with the help of it, a god is supposed to confer Buddha-hood or success upon his worshipper.[18]

Thus, the Vajrayāna or Taṅtrayāna on the whole, does not appear to be a religion, but an admixture of philosophy, science, superstition, dogmas, psychic exercises and mysticism dealing with subjects like *yōga*, *haṭhayōga*, prognosis, divination, astrology, medicine, alchemy, horoscopy, chirognomy etc.

According to Tārānath, Tāṅtricism flourished secretly since the time of Asanga (3rd c. A.D.) to Dharmakirti (5th-6th c. A.D.) whence its followers increased numerically i.e. from 3rd c. A.D. onwards, and it came out openly to preach the essence of the doctrine.[19] The term *Taṅtra* occurs for the first time in the Gangadhara stone inscription of the time of Kumara Gupta dated in the Malwa year 480 (A.D. 523-24).[20] The important philosophers were Saraha, Lupia, Padmavajra, Anangavajra, Nagarjuna, Lilāvajra, Jālandharipa, Darikapā, Guhya, Vijāyapā, Taipā, Nāropā and Indrabhuti who were not only the *Mahāsiddhas* but also great authors of magic and *Taṅtra*.[21]

*Guhya Siddhi* of Padmavajra and the *Jñāna Siddhi* of Indrabhuti are the important works on Tāṅtricism. Of the two, the former is in the original *Saṅgītī* which introduced the tenets of Vajrayāna into orthoox Buddhism and is considered as one of the nine *Dharaṇis* of Nepal.[22] The other works are *Mañjuśrī Mūla Kalpa, Tattva Saṅgraha* of Santārākṣita, *Amitaya Sutra* or *Sukhavate Sūtra*, *Niṣpannayōgāvaḷi* of Mahāpandita Abhayakaragupta (1084-1130 A.D.), *Sādhanamāla* (1165 A.D.), *Tattvaratnāvali* of Advaya Vajra (12th c. A.D.) in addition to other works like *Kriyā Samuccaya* and the *Vajravali-nāmamaṇḍalopayika*.[23]

It is not known exactly from which region the doctrine of Vajrayāna originated. According to *Sādhanamāla* (12th-13th c. A.D.) its important centres are Kāmākhya (Kamarupa), Sirihaṭṭa (Assam), Pūrṇagiri and Uddiyāna. The Tibetan authorities say that Tāṅtricism originated from Uddiyāna (Vajra Yōgini) and from there, it was propagated to the other parts of India.[24] It appears that the early tenets of Vajrayāna were preached by Āchārya Nāgārjuna at Nagarjunakonda (Śrīparvata) in Andhra Pradesh. Though no clear evidence is available in support of the above hypothesis, there are literary and archaeological evidences to attest to the early beginnings of Vajrayāna school of philosophy at Dharaṇikōṭa and Nagarjunakonda in Andhra Pradesh.

According to the *Kathāvathu*, the *chaityakas* were responsible for elevating the Buddha as *Lōkōttārā*.[25] The *Chaityakas* or *Andhakas* among the *Saila* schools of Āndhradēśa developed the *Pāramita* literature which deals with the deities, *Mantras* and *Dharaṇis*. This led to the rise of the concept of *Dharmadhātu,* a sort of Buddhist priest. For offering worship, certain tenets were developed, such as circumambulation, offering flowers and garlands, lamps, incense etc. To perform these rituals, they needed a preceptor which was of a fundamental importance to Vajrayāna Buddhism.[26] These primitive innovations developed by the *Chaityakas,* might have inspired the Tāntricists to follow.

The *Nikāya Saṁgraha*, a Ceylonese Buddhist text, refers to a sect called *Vajraparvatavāsinikāya* probably residing at *Vajraparvata*.[27] Scholars identified this *Vajraparvata* with *Śrīparvata* where Āchārya Nagarjuna taught the essence of *Mādhyamika* school of philosophy. Probably the medieval Ceylonese Buddhist texts mentions *Śrīparvata* as Vajraparvata since the Vajrayāna principles were formulated at Nagarjunakonda. According to tradition, a monk by name Dasavala deposited *Mantra Tantra-kāla chakra* and *Dharaṇis* at Dhānyakaṭaka and hence the place came to be known as 'Dharaṇikōṭa' or the 'fort of *Dharaṇis*'.[38] Hieun Tsang in his account mentions that there was a temple dedicated to Vajrapāṇi at Dharaṇikōṭa where monks, desirous of supernatural powers, recited the Vajrapāṇi *dharani*. It indicates that by the time Hieun-Tsang visited the place, Dharaṇikōṭa became a centre for the production of spells and exorcisms.[29] A Tibetan account mentions a king by name *Srong Tsangam - Po* (7th c. A.D.) brought an eleven headed image of Avalōkitēśwara from Potalaka in South India.[30] Scholars are of the opinion that the place Potalaka stood on the banks of the river Krishna near Dhānyakaṭaka. There, it appears that before 6th c. A.D. itself Dhānyakaṭaka stood as a prominent centre for Vajrayāna Buddhism.

Interestingly, a pot sherd from Salihundam—a Buddhist site in Andhra Pradesh, datable to 4th c. A.D. incised in Brahmi characters reads as *Pañca(vīra)* i.e. the five *vīras* or the five *Dhyāni* Buddhas.[31] The discovery of several Vajrayāna images at this place confirms that this settlement flourished not only as a famous Vajrayāna Buddhist centre in north coastal Andhradēśa but also suggests the early beginnings of Vajrayāna Buddhism in Āndhradēśa. Another inscription engraved on the pedestal of a Buddha image from Jaggayyapeta refers to Bhadanta Nagarjuna. The inscription is in Sanskrit language and reads as :[32]

*Svasti, Bhadanta Nāgārjunāchāryasya*
*Sishya(ḥ) Jaya PrabhĀchārya(ḥ) tachhishyēna cha(ndra).*

*Prabhena Kara pitam, Satya-sugata gala Prasāda Viṣeśa Viśiṣṭa saṁsāre divamanu (ja).*
*Vibhūti pūrvakaṁ Buddhatva Prāpti nimittaṁ Buddha Pratimaṁ Pratishṭāpitam anumōdanāṁ (Pakshe)*
*Kurvantu Sarvē angatyagr aya(?) nyopi.*

The meaning of the inscription is that 'Chandraprabha, the disciple of Jaya Prabha who in turn was the disciple of Bhadanta Nagarjunāchārya, after the enjoyment of greatness in the worlds of gods and men in the course of existences characterised by the favours of the Buddha caused His *Pratima* to be installed for the attainment of Buddha-hood. May everybody including *Parama Saugatas* approve the image.' On paleographical grounds the inscription is datable to 5th-6th c. A.D. Nāgārjuna mentioned in the inscription is identical with Siddha Nāgārjuna, who preached Tāntricism in Āndhradēśa during 5th-6th c. A.D.

Another inscription from Dhānyakaṭaka refers to a Pallava king named Simhavarman II, who visited Dhānyakaṭaka and listened to a discourse on the law in a secluded place.[33] Hieun-Tsang also confirms that Dhānyakaṭaka was a centre for the worship of Vajrapāṇi and *Dharaṇis*.[34]

After Nagarjuna, Āryadēva and Bhāvavivēka were the great teachers of *Śūnyavāda*. Diṅgnāga and Dharmakirti were responsible for the development of Yōgacāra school of philosophy in Āndhradēśa. Diṅgnāga was the author of *Prajñā Pāramita Saṁgraha* in which he gave an exposition of the concept of *advaya*. Vajrabōdhi Dharmpāla, Buddhamitra and Dharmakīrti were some of the teachers who spread Vajrayāna literature in Tamilnadu.

Thus, the above literary and archaeological evidences amply support that Vajrayāna Buddhism began around 4th-5th c. A.D. or even before in South India at several places, particularly in Dhānyakaṭaka and Nagarjunkonda in Andhra Pradesh and it was from these centres, Tāntricism travelled to other parts of India as also to South East Asian countries through coastal Āndhradēśa.

## REFERENCES


1. Christmas Humphreys, *Buddhism,* Great Britain, 1954, p. 54.
2. S. Tripathi, *Guhya Samaja Tantra (Tathāgata Guhyak),* Sanskrit series No. 9, Darbanga, 1988, pp. I to X.
3. S.B. Das Gupta, *An introduction to Tāntric Buddhism,* Calcutta, 1950, pp. 9-10.
4. A.A.G. Bennet, "The Sukhavati literature" *Sambhasha-Mahā Bodhi centenary commemorative volume,* Vol. I., No. 2, 1991, pp. 243-252.
5. B. Bhattacharya, *The Indian Buddhist Iconography,* Calcutta, 1968, pp. 8-9.
6. Peter Della Santina, *The Tree of Enlightenment,* Taiwan, 1997, pp. 100-101.
7. W. Zwalf, *Buddhism, Art & Faith,* pp. 17-18.
8. B. Bhattacharya, *Op.cit.,* 1968, p. 9.
9. Heramba Chatterjee, 'An introduction to Yōgacāra School' *Sambhasha-Mahā Bodhi Centenary Commemorative Volume,* Vol. I, No. 2, 1991, pp. 238-239.
10. Peter Della Santina, *Op. cit.*, 1997, pp. 100-113.
11. B. Bhattacharya, *Op.cit.,* 1968, p.31.
12. B. Bhattacharya, *An introduction to Buddhist Esoterism,* 1980, pp. 120-21.
13. N.K. Bhattasali, *Iconography of Buddhist and Brāhmanical sculptures in the Dacca Museum,* Delhi, 1972, pp. 16-19.
14. B. Bhattacharya, *Op.cit.,* 1980, pp. 83-86.
15. B. Bhattacharya, *Op.cit.,* 1968, pp. 25-26.
16. *Ibid.*, pp. 27-28.
17. *Ibid.,* p. 29.
18. *Ibid,* p. 391.
19. Alice Gettey, *The Gods of the Northern Buddhism,* 1978, p. XXIX
20. V.R. Mani, *Sapta Mātṛikas in Indian Religion and Art,* Delhi, 1995, p. 83.
21. B. Bhattacharya, *Op.cit.,* pp. 63-65.
22. S. Tripathi, *Op.cit.,* 1985, pp. I-X.
23. B. Bhattacharya, *Op.cit.,* 1968, pp.12-14.
24. B. Bhattacharya, *Op.cit.,* 1980, 43.
25. B.S.L. Hanumantha Rao, *Religion in Andhra,* Hyderabad, 1993, p. 127.
26. B. Bhattacharya, *Op.cit.,* 1968, p. XVII.
27. L.M. Joshi, 'Original Home of Tāntric Buddhism', *Journnal of Oriental Institute*, Vol. XVI, pp. 223-232.
28. K.R. Subramanian, *Buddhist Remains in Andhra,* Delhi, p. 31.
29. Rhys Davids T.W., *Thomas Watter's on Hieun Tsang Travels in India,* Delhi, 1961, p. II, p. 215.

30. R. C.Mitra, *Decline of Buddhism in India,* Viswabharati, 1954, p. 104.
31. R. Subrahmanyam, *Salihundam,* Hyderabad, 1964, pp. 51-52.
32. J. Burgess, *The Buddhist Stūpas of Amaravati and Jaggayyapeta,* London, 1887, p. 112.
33. H. Hultzsch, 'A Pallava inscription at Amaravati', *South Indian Inscriptions,* Vol. I, Delhi, 1987, pp. 154-59.
34. Rhys Davids T.W., *Op.cit.,* 1961, p. 215.

# VAJRYĀNA BUDDHIST CENTRES

South India for purpose of the present study, comprises the States of Andhra Pradesh, Tamilnadu, Pondicherry, Karnataka and Kerala. These states were once, partly or completely included in the territory of the Mauryan king Aśōka (3rd c. B.C.) which fact is also attested to by his edicts No.II and XIII. The rock edict No.II mentions the southern kingdoms such as the Chola (the Coromandal coast), the Pandya (the southern tip of the peninsula), Kerala or Cheradesa (Malabar) and the land of Satyaputras (a part of Tamilnadu) which were the border states of the Mauryan empire.[1] The discovery of Aśōkan edicts at Eṛṛagudi and Rajula Mandagiri in Andhra Pradesh and Brahmagiri, Siddapur and Maski in Karnataka obviously suggests that these regions also formed part of Aśōka's dominions. Further the XIII rock edict of Aśōka, refers to the people of Āndhradēśa as living in his dominion along with others who were scrupulously following the *Dhamma.*[2]

After the third Buddhist council under Moggaliputta Tissa held in Aśōka's presence at Pataliputra, several Bhikkus were sent to different parts of India and also to Ceylon for the propagation of Buddhism. The Pali tradition also advert clearly to Aśōka's Buddhist missions to South India under Mahādeva and Rakkita sent by the emperor to Mahiṣamaṇḍala (Maisolia region) and Vanavāsi (Karnataka).[3] Thus Aśōka was mainly instrumental for introducing Buddhism or *Dhamma* in South India. But archaeological evidences from Bhattiprolu (Rāja Kuberaka)[4], Vaddamanu (Rāja Sōmaka)[5] and Amaravati (Rāja Kumaria Sammaliya)[6] in Āndhradēśa, suggest that the local kings were responsible for patronising Buddhism in their respective regions and also propagating it to contiguous regions prior to the propagation of Buddhism by Aśōka. The recent discovery of the portrait sculpture of Aśōka with his wife and attendants at Kanganahalli near Sannati in Karnataka State, is another important evidence which support the visit of the Mauryan emperor Aśōka to the marvellous *Mahāstūpa* and monastic complex at Kanganahalli.[7] Thus, the above evidences undoubtedly confirm that the South Indian Buddhism was pre-Aśōkan. However it is only after the conquest of Kalinga, Aśōka took the *Dhamma* and propagated it to all over the sub-continent on a large scale as his religious mandate. *(Dhamma Vijaya)*

For all reasons, it was South-India which provided a firm foothold for nourishment of Buddhism for over a period of two thousand years, owing largely to its geographical situation along the coast as well as the existence of several prosperous and fertile river basins, such as the Kaveri basin in Tamilnadu; the Bhima-Tungabhadra basin in Karnataka; and the Krishna-Godavari and the Vamsadhara-Tandava basins in Andhra Pradesh. During the early centuries of Christian era, the people of South-India seemed to have embraced Buddhism quite early when compared to other parts of India and also patronised and supported its existence for longer duration i.e. upto the post-Vijayanagara period (17th c.A.D.). On the whole, Buddhism had a good beginning particularly in South India since at least Aśōkan times.

Though scholars are of the opinion that Buddhism disappeared with the Mahāyāna phase in South India, in fact it was the Vajrayāna phase of Buddhism during 4th-5th c.A.D. that took reins of the sunken tenets of Buddhism and guided running its fortunes upto the medieval period, parallel to Vedic Brahmanism. Archaeological evidences at Dhānyakaṭaka, Salihundam, Guntupalli, Gummadidurru, Sankaram etc. in Andhra Pradesh; Kanchipuram, Kaveripattanam, Nagapattanam in Tamilnadu and Sannati, Kanganahalli and Kadri in Karnataka proved beyond doubt that Vajrayāna Buddhism flourished for longer duration i.e. upto 14th-16th c. A.D. in the South when compared to the north (Map. I). The Vajrayāna centres in South India are characterised by the presence of the sculptural representation of the five *Dhyāni* Buddhas with their consorts, Bodhisattvas, inscribed clay tablets containing *Dharaṇis* or *Maṅtras*, inscribed bronze icons and stone sculptures of various Gods and Godesses along with Buddhist creed formulae.

It is necessary to study the Vajrayāna Buddhist centres in South India in their proper chronological context not only to understand the emergence of Vajrayāna, its phenomenal growth, development, spread and survival and its impact on the contemporary religions but also to know the beginnings of cult dieties besides other developments in the fields of art and iconography, philosophy, Sanskrit literature etc.

## ANDHRA PRADESH

The early structural monuments of the Buddhist period built of lime plastered brick walls and ornamented with stucco work are spread over a vast area from Neelavati in the north to Nandalur in the south-west, Ghantasala and Kanuparthy on the east to Kōṭaliṅgāla and Kondapur on the north-west in Andhra Pradesh. A number of Thēravāda (Hinayāna) Buddhist sites were located in north coastal Andhra, whereas the Mahāyāna sites were predominant in mid coastal Andhra, especially in the fertile tract lying between the rivers Godavari and Krishna. Till recently, scholars held the opinion that, it was only due to the untiring efforts and missisonary zeal of the great Mauryan emperor Aśōka, that Buddhism entered Āndhradēśa and grew into a State religion. Undoubtedly the Buddhism in Andhra was pre-Aśōkan as evidenced by recent archaeological discoveries from various parts of Andhra Pradesh which have thrown fresh light on various aspects of Buddhism, especially its patronization by the local kings or chieftains in Āndhradēśa even before the propagation of Buddhism by Aśōka. Candidly speaking, Aśōka was instrumental in propagating the religion on a large scale, as a part of his religious expedition i.e. *dhamma vijaya*, soon after the conquest of Kalinga.

There is also a well known episode of a Brahmana sage Bavari of Kosala, who lived at a place called *Kavitavana* on the banks of the river Godavari, near Assaka region in Dakṣināpatha and in the peripheral areas of Mulaka who sent his pupils to Rājagriha, to meet the Buddha and learn his teachings.[8] According to *Lalita Vistārā*, an actor from Dakṣināpatha, performed a drama narrating the story of Lord Buddha, along with other artists, in the presence of a king named Bindusāra who was a contemporary of the great Master.[9] According to *Vimānavatthu*, Mahākātyayāna, the chief disciple of Lord Buddha, preached Buddha *Dharma* to the king of Assaka.[10]

The *Suttanipata* also states that the *Janapadas* of Assaka and Mulaka were located in *Dakṣināpatha*. The region of Assaka corresponding to Pliny's Asmagai i.e. Assaka includes the present districts of Karimnagar, Nizamabad and Warangal in Andhra Pradesh with its capital at Potali, i.e. modern Bodhan in Nizamabad district. Recent survey in this region resulted in the discovery of an ancient city locally known as 'Kōṭaliṅgāla' on the left bank of the river Godavari in Karimnagar district, where excavations unearthed a well fortified township, in addition to monastic and non-monastic structures and a wide range of early historic antiquities such as coins, beads, iron implements, glass bangles and terracotta figurines, a large quantity of ceramic wares such as black and red, red slipped, red polished, grey and black polished. This probably was the place where the hermitage of the sage Bavari stood, for, it was situated in Kaviṭavana on the banks of the river Godavari. The word Kaviṭa in Telugu language means 'Velaga' (name of a fruit-wood apple) and the existence of a village named 'Velagatur' or Yelkatur in close vicinity to Kōṭaliṅgāla township lends credence to the above view. Further, interestingly enough, from this place, a good number of coins belonging to pre-Sātavāhana kings like Gōbhada, Kaṅvāyasiri, Samagōpa, Nārana and Silver punch marked coins of Mauryan times were noticed in clear stratigraphical context.[11]

In the early centuries of Christian era, Āndhradēśa was divided into several petty States or minor principalities, ruled by local chieftains or *Rājas*. During this period, it was these kings, who mainly patronized and propagated Buddhism even to the outlying or far flung areas of their territories, as evidenced by the existence of numerous Buddhist sites along the coast and on the banks of major rivers. Among them, mention may be made of the kings assignable to the pre-Sātavāhana times. They are Rāño Gōbhada, Rāño Kaṁvāyaśiri, Rāño Nārana and Rāño Samagōpa, who ruled over the tract lying between the rivers Godavari and Maneru in northern Telingana region with its capital at Kōṭaliṅgāla.[12] The next local king that we know of, was Rāja Kuberaka, who ruled over the tract situated along the south-east coast of Andhra, with Bhattiprolu, as its capital city.[13] He, according to the relic casket inscription, was responsible for constructing the *Mahā Chaitya*, enshrining the corporeal relics of the Buddha. Other local kings that we find are Sōmaka mentioned in an inscription at Vaddamanu near Amaravati[14] and Rāja Kumariyya Sammliya, from Amaravati,[15] where vestiges of an ancient Buddhist settlement, along with a number of punch-marked coins were brought to light.

The discovery of a fragmentary Aśōkan pillar edict in association with N.B.P. ware and other early historic cultural material at Amaravati, obviously suggest the wide prevalance of Buddhism in Āndhradēśa.[16] Mauryan hegemony over Andhra region can be seen only in the peripheral areas of the south-western parts of Āndhradēśa, which is attested to by the discovery of minor rock edicts of Aśōka at Joṇṇagiri or Eṛṛagudi[17] and Rājulamaṅdagiri[18] in Kurnool district. The non-occurrence of Aśōkan edicts in coastal Āndhradēśa, except for a solitary fragment at Amaravati and in Telingana and some parts of Rāyalaseema areas, clearly suggests that these fertile and prosperous tracts were ruled by the local *Rājas* or chieftains.

After the downfall of the Mauryan empire, all the subordinate kings declared themselves as autonomous rulers of various territories. In Āndhradēśa, the period of Sātavāhana rule (B.C. 200 to 200 A.D.) witnessed the growth and development of Buddhism and Buddhist art, besides maritime trade. Under their rule, the religious tenets set forth by the kings were scrupulously followed by major sections of the society, which helped the spread of Buddhism to every segment of the State. Buddhist institutions received munificent grants and it was well supported by the royalty.

After the Sātavāhanas, Buddhism continued to receive patronage by their successors, namely Ikṣvāku, Śālaṅkāyana, Viṣṇukuṇḍin and other minor dynasties, who, however, were staunch adherents of Brāhmanical religion. The famous Buddhist centre at Vijayapuri i.e. modern Nagarjunakonda became the cradle of Mahāyāna Buddhism under the Ikṣvāku rulers and it attracted the attention of kings and missionaries from far off regions like Ceylon, Kāshmir, Gāndhāra, China, Chilate, Tosali, Aparanta, Vaṅga, Vanavāsi, Yavana and Draviḍa as attested by the epigraphs found at the site.[19] The Mayidavolu charters of Pallava Śiva Skandavarman (300 A.D.) mention Dhānyakaṭaka as the headquarters of *Āndhrapātha*,[20] which shows that it was also under the controle of the Ikṣvāku rulers for quite sometime, as also confirmed by the recently discovered Kallacheruvu copper plates[21] (1998, preserved in A.P.State Museum, Hyderabad).

During the post-Ikṣvāku times, with the revival of Brāhmanical faith, patronage for Buddhism declined to a low ebb. Royal support which was its mainstay witnessed a downward trend. However, its survival as a religion, in some parts of Āndhradēśa continued even upto the late medieval times. The Śālankāyanas, Anandagōtrins, Viṣṇukuṇḍis and other minor dynasties that ruled over different parts of Āndhradēśa during 4-5th centuries A.D., played considerable role in the spread of Buddhism to different parts of India and South-East Asian countries.

The subsequent rulers who ruled over different parts of Āndhradēśa were strong supporters of Brāhmanical religion. Further, the infiltration of Vajrayāna, with great emphasis on the female element and large scale practice of *Tāntric* Buddhism, led to laxity in discipline and moral fervour.[22] The *Mattavilāsa prahasana* of Pallava Mahendravarman describes in detail the detestable lives led by the contemporary Buddhists.[23] Further, there was pronounced tendency towards the creation of *Śaktis* or consorts to the Bōdhisattvas. This resulted in the creation of a mystic sex symbolism and objectionable and immoral practices. For the above reasons, most of the institutions have lost their importance, particularly in the direction of sanctity and that was why, the people of later times called these deserted settlements as *Lanja Dibbalau* (whore's mounds), particularly in Andhra Pradesh.

Yet, some important sites like Dhānyakaṭaka, Salihundam and Gummadidurru continued to flourish even upto the medieval times, under the patronage of minor local dynasties like Kota chiefs of Dharaṇikōṭa.[24] The Bekkallu grant of Chalukya Tribhuvanamalladeva dated 1100 A.D. refers to the construction of temples for Śiva, Viṣṇu, Jina and Buddha at Bekkallu in Jangaon taluk of Warangal district.[25] The Korni plates of Anantavarma Choda Ganga deva (12th c.A.D.) describe the Buddhist site at Salihundam (*mundu marru*) as a famous place of *mundiya* monks[26] (clean shaven monks). The Gadaladeniya, inscription of Ceylon refers to certain renovation works attended to by Dhammakīrti, a *Thera* from Ceylon, at Dhānya-kaṭaka.[27] The occurrence of clay tablets at Gummadidurru, bearing Buddhist creed formulae in Nagari script, datable to late medieval period, suggests the survival of Buddhism upto 14th-15th c.A.D. in Andhra Pradesh.

Archaeological studies reveal that the Buddhist sites in Āndhradēśa bear marks of the evolutionary growth of Buddhism in all the three phases i.e. Thērvāda, Mahāyāna and Vajrayāna and endured till 14th century A.D. Some of the early Buddhist centres like Thotlakonda, Pavuralakonda, Nandalur, Penumaka, Chandavaram etc. which flourished as Thēravāda centres remained as Theravādic throughout until they faded into oblivion. Some centres such as Ghantasala, Buddham, Alluru etc. basing on the tenets of Mahāyāna continued for a longer period and ended abruptly uninfluenced by Vajrayānism. Yet other sites like Nelakondapalli, Gummadidurru and Sankaram which began with Mahāyāna phase of Buddhism later on passed on to the Vajrayāna. Guntupalli, Dhānyakaṭaka and Salihundam witnessed all the three phases namely Thēravāda, Mahāyāna and finally Vajrayāna Buddhism till their gradual disappearance.

The Vajrayāna Buddhist centres in Āndhradēśa were characterised by the presence of sculptures like Bōdhisattvas, various Gods and Goddesses, inscribed clay tablets and inscriptions on stone sculptures and icons which contain *Dharaṇis* or *Mantras*. Important centres like Gopalapatnam, Ramatirtham, Sankaram, Nagarjunakonda, Amaravati, Salihundam, Guntupalli, Gummadidurru etc. provide glimpses of Vajrayāna phase of Buddhism in Āndhradēśa.

## GOPALAPATNAM

It is a small village situated on the left bank of river Tandava in Payakaraopeta mandal of Visakhapatnam district. It lies about 10 kms. south of Tuni railway station on Visakhapatnam-Vijayawada section of South Central Railway. It can be approached by bus from Tuni or Payakaraopeta. Survey in and around the village revealed traces of brick structures like circular *stūpas*, stone veneered *stūpas*, *vihāras* and sculptural fragments such as *chhatra* pieces, stone plaques, tiles and early historic materials both in the habitation as well as on the flat summits of the hill ranges, locally known as Bubhikonda, Sitammakonda, Burelametta and Veerulametta. There are also rock-cut caves on the ledge of the Bubhikonda hillock. It appears that the present village has been built over the ancient habitation. Excavations in the habitation site brought to light brick built votive *stūpas* and pottery assignable to Sātavāhana times. While removing debris from the *pradakṣaṇapatha*, one of the votive *stūpas* belonging to post-Sātavāhana levels yielded sculptured stone plaques such as nude Mother Goddess, musician and a standing male figure holding a *khaṭvāṅga* and pointed *vajra* in the hands.[29] The last mentioned plaque is identifiable with Heruka of the Vajrayāna Pantheon. The discovery of the image of Mother Goddess along with Heruka of Vajrayāna Buddhism needs critical study.

**Heruka :** This image was carved out of red sand stone, with four hands and standing in *samabhanga* pose on a pedestal. The sculpture is much weathered. The left arm and the lower right hand portions are broken. On examination, it was found that he holds a *vajra* in his right hand with its pointed end facing upwards and a *khaṭvāṅga,* with a jewel crest on the top of the skull, in his left hand. In the right and left lower hands he hold a sword and a bowl. He wears a conical head-gear and elaborate earlobes (Pl. 1c). The iconographical features of the image tally with the description of Heruka as given in the *Sādhanamāla*. He occupied a prominent place in the family of Akṣobhya. A similar limestone image, depicted with two hands was reported from Amaravati.

The worship of Heruka is said to confer Buddha-hood on his worshippers and he is said to destroy all the evils or Maras of the world. Several *dhyānas* are mentioned both in the *Niṣpannayōgāvali* and *Sādhanamāla*.[30]

## RAMATIRTHAM

It is a road side village on the Ongole-Podili high-way and is 30 kms. away from Ongole in Prakasam district. Exploration near Chimakurti hill in the outskirts of Ramatirtham village revealed a Buddhist site, littered with large sized bricks and early historic pottery such as red ware, black polished ware and decorated sherds datable to 2nd century A.D. The sculpture of Bōdhisattva Avalōkitēśvara found near the Moksharamalingeswara temple is said to have been recovered from the disturbed Buddhist settlement, in the slopes of the hill[31].

**Ávalōkitēśvara :** This standing lime stone image has two hands, holding a lotus in the right hand and an ornamental mace in the left. The image is profusely decorated with *kirīṭamakuṭa, makara kuṇḍalas, graivēyaka, udarabandha, sarpakēyuras, prakōṣṭa-valayas* and prominent *yajñōpavīta* (Pl. 2). The depiction of the under-garment with dangling tassels in the centre is a feature commonly found in the sculptures of Amaravati and Nagarjunakonda. A unique iconographical feature is prescribed in the *Dharmadhātu Vāgīśvara* as follows :[32]

*Avalōkitēśvaraḥ, Śubhrah Saveyena*
*Varado Vāmena Sarōjadharaḥ*

'The God is of white colour and represented with two hands. He holds the lotus in his left hand, while the right hand is in *varada mudrā.'*

Generally, Avalōkitēśvara is known in Buddhist literature as Bōdhisattva Padmapāṇi, the spiritual son of the *Dhyāni* Buddha Amitābha. A compassionate

Bōdhisattva looks upon the suffering world and offers deliverance to sentient beings.He has 108 different forms. The *Sādhanamāla* describes fifteen forms in thirty eight *sādhanās*. In the *Macchandar Vahal* of Khatmandu (Nepal) 108 forms are painted[33]. It is the earliest deity among the *dharaṇis*.

There are various opinions about the origin of this God. A Tibetan text, the '*Manikambum*' says that Amitābha, after giving himself upto earnest meditation, caused a white ray of light to emanate from his right eye, which resulted in the emergence of Padmapāṇi (Avalōkitēśvara)[34]. In the *Guṇakāranda Vyūha* (4th c. A.D) he is the glorified God who issued out of the primordial Buddha (*Ādi* Buddha)[35].

In the *Dharmakōśa Saṅgraha* two forms are described, one is *Sukhavati Lōkēśvara,* having a *chaitya* on the top of his crown and the other is *Uṣṇīṣavijayā* having a *chaitya* itself as crown (*Chaitya Chūdāmaṇi*)[36]. The *Kāranda-Vyūha* mentions that in later ages numerous divinities emanated out of this deity. From the eyes of this God emerged, the Sun and the Moon, Mahēśvara from forehead, Brahma from the shoulders, Nārāyaṇa from the ears, Saraswati from the two rows of teeth, *Vāyu* (air) from the mouth, *Pṛithvī* (Earth) from the feet, *Varuṇa* (water) from the abdomen, *Vāhini* from the navel and Lakṣmī and Śrī from the left and right thighs[37].

As a non-Tāntric form, he was worshipped right from the Aśōkan times. He became prominent only since 4th century A.D. Tārā, the consort of the God, appears in the sculptures, only from 6th-7th centuries A.D onwards. She was given the status of mother-hood for all the Buddhas. In the early sculptures we do not find any sculptural representation of this Goddess as the consort of the God. The sculpture under study appears to be the earliest form of the God Avalōkitēśwara though the image is devoid of the effigy of Amitābha in his crown (taira) and representation of his consort Tārā.

Hieun-Tsang mentions Potalaka (white flower mountain) as the favourite resort of Avalōkitēśvara[38]. Tārānatha says that several pious Buddhists paid visit to the Bōdhisattva. Alice Getty says that Avalōkitēśvara was dwelling on the mount Potalaka before manifesting himself in China in the form of a female deity, Kuan-yin[39]. He located the place Potalaka in South-India. Scholars are of the opinion that the place Potalaka might be in the region of Dhanyakata or Etthipothala near the mouths of the river Krishna in Andhra. But it is difficult to identify the place precisely in the present state of our knowledge. It is not known why Avalōkitēśvara is particularly associated with the Mount Potalaka.

## SANKARAM

The twin hillocks, locally known as Bojjanakonda and Lingalametta, lies to the north of Anakapalle at a distance of 3 kms. near the village Sankaram, a corrupt form of *Saṅghārāmam.* The rivulet Sarada flows by the side of village, which is the principal water source for both trade and drinking. The hillocks were for the first time noticed by Alexander Rea (1907-08) which were elegantly dotted with a row of rock cut votive *stūpas,* resembling '*Śiva liṅgas*' and hence, familiarly known as Lingalametta. On the top of the other hillock Bojjanakonda, lies the main *stūpa*, and host of brick built votive *stūpas, vihāras*, rock cut cells, apsidal rock cut shrines etc. The main *stūpa* consists of a square platform (80" × 11'9") approached by a flight of steps, a drum (64'8" dia×7' 6" high) and a dome (60'8" dia) commanding a panoramic view of the fertile country side[40].

Excavations yielded several clay tablets, conical and square seal impressions bearing figures of seated Buddha, Pagodas and Buddhist creed formulae (Pl. 3). Some of the globular seals contain impressions of *mantras*. Other antiquities recovered from the site include seventy copper coins of the Eastern Chalukyan dynasty (7th c. A.D), one lead coin bearing the figure of horse (Sātavāhana coin), one gold coin of Samudrāgupta, images of Buddha etc. Basing on the architectural features of the monastic complex and other early historic cultural material, the beginnings of the site may be assigned to 2nd-3rd centuries A.D. and it flourished upto 9th-10 centuries A.D.

The eastern side of hillock is perched with brick structures, whereas the western and northern sides of the summit are concentrated with scooped out caves. The caves on the western side, which are wider and larger in dimension contain exquisitely carved Buddhist sculptures. Caves No. 4 and 5 on the northern slope are lesser in dimension. Cave no. 5, rectangular on plan, is an important one, as it contains ornate pillars, sculptures of Buddha in *Dhyānamudrā* (Pl. 4), *Bōdhisattvas* and other tāntric deities[41]. Other important sculptures found were the Goddess Harītī and a tāntric form of Gaṇapati.

**Harītī** : The image of Harītī (1.42 × 0.91 mtrs.) locally known as *Palakamma* is represented with two arms, seated on a lotus pedestal in *lalitāsana*. Her left hand holds the child astride on her left lap, while the right hand is kept in *vitarka mudrā*. A round object held in the left hand of the child, may be identified as the fruit, pomegranate. Five children depicted on either side of her head, symbolise her 500 sons as mentioned in the Buddhist literature. She is flanked by two chowry bearers standing in *tribhaṅga* attitude. She has a decorated conical head-gear, covered by a thin cloth, the hanging folds of which are seen on the shoulder. It is profusely ornamented with *karnikā mallika, kuḍmāla, kēyūras, nūpuras, kaṇṭhimukta yajñōpavīta, prakōṣṭhavalayas* etc., she is shown with prominent undergarment tied up with a waist band, the tassels of which hang down in the centre. Represented elegantly, gracefully and pleasingly, the depiction seems to suggest motherly countenance (Pl. 5).

Several stories abound about the origin of the goddess in Buddhist literature. According to *Mahāvāstu*[42], there lived a *Yakṣiṇi* by name Kuṇḍala (Harītī) in the sub-Himālayan regions. Every year, she gave birth to 100 children and thus begot 500 children. Afterwards she died when the number of children reached 1000. The story is not clearly mentioned in the text.

The *Vinaya Pīṭaka of Sarvāsti-Vāda School* says that there was a Yakṣiṇi by name Huanshi (which means 'joy') supposed to be the guardian deity of Magadha. Due to a spiteful wish in her previous life, she took to stealing and eating the children of Rājagriha. As a result, she was given the name Harītī by the people of Rājagriha, for the term 'Harītī' means 'thief'. After hearing the plea from the people, Buddha undertook to put an end to Yakṣiṇi's diabolical nature. It is said that Buddha hid her youngest son Pingala in his alms bowl and offered it to Harītī to eat. Realising this, with horror what she was about to do, she changed her attitude and converted herself to become a lay disciple of the Buddha. In turn, for the subsistence of Harītī and her children, the Buddha instructed the inhabitants to provide food to them. From that day onwards all the monasteries kept food aside for her every morning. Ever since she and her children became guardians of the monasteries[43].

In the *Saṁyukta vāstu*[44], Harītī, otherwise known as Abhirati was the sister of Satogiri, the protector of Rājagriha. She married Panduka, the son of Pañchala, the Yakṣa protector of Gāndhāra. She had five children, youngest son was Priyankara. The story of conversion of Yakṣiṇi by the Buddha is the same as (Harītī) described in *Vinayapīṭakaṁ*. The *Bōdhisattvāvadana-Kalpalatā* of Kṣēmēndra[45] mentions her son's name as Priyankara. To change her cannibal mode of life, Buddha offered her a red pomegranate, as the inner core of the fruit looks like mutton of human flesh. In the *Saṁyukta-ratna-sūtra* of the Chinese *Sūtra Pīṭaka* of the Hinayāna school, the youngest son of Harītī was Pingala or Pilingika. It described her as a protectress and giver of children.[46]

Itsing mentioned in his book *viz.*, '*A record of the Buddhist religion in India*' that Harītī was not only the giver of children but also of wealth. He says that the sculpture of Harītī holding a baby in her arms and with children playing around her was found in the porch or in a corner of the dining hall of all the Indian monasteries[47]. In a Tibetan manuscript, the *sādhana* mentioned her as red in colour with *nakula* in her hand. Holding a *nakula* signifies her as the bestower of wealth[48].

A beautiful bronze image of Harītī datable to 1st-2nd centuries A.D. was reported from Dhulikatta, a Buddhist site in Karimnagar district[49]. She is seated on a pedestal with legs dangling in *bhadrāsana*. She holds a baby in her left hand while the right hand rests on her knee. There is a round object in the right hand of the child which probably is a pomegranate. The image is crudely made without delineating clear iconographical features. The hair, eyes, mouth and ornaments such as ear rings, necklaces, amulets, bracelets, waist band and the *mēkhala* were crudely carved in applique design (Pl. 6). This is the earliest bronze icon of Harītī reported so far from South India.

Another sculpture of Harītī comes from Karkaipalle village near Elamanchili in Visakhapatnam district[50]. She is depicted with two hands and seated on a pedestal. She holds a baby in her right hand, while her left hand is kept in *varada mudrā*. The sculpture is mutilated (Pl. 7). She is decked with ornaments. Her hair is drawn aside and made into double bun. Interestingly, a standing lion is depicted below the folded left leg on the pedestal (Pl. 7). This is a unique sculpture depicted with a *vāhana* for the goddess. On iconographical features, it is dated to 10th-11th centuries A.D.

Though Harītī, as a deity, is found in the early Buddhist literature, her worship came into vogue only after the advent of Mahāyānism. Generally, she is represented with two arms. However, an image representing four hands with a skull cup and fish and holding a baby with her two hands is, now in the Decca Museum. The depiction of the goddess (*Ātavaka*) with a skull cup and sword suggests the cannibalic nature of the deity[51].

Chinese worship this goddess with the name Kui-tzu-mushen (mother of Demon sons[52]). She is depicted as standing, with a baby in her arms and two or three children below her knees. She is the only goddess in Buddhist pantheon who holds a baby in her hands. The father of her children was the Yakṣa Pāñchika, one of the twenty eight generals in the Yakṣa army of Vaiśravana (Kubera). A warrior holding a lance by the side of Harītī surrounded by many children is often found in the Gandhara sculptures. At Sahri-Bahal and Takt-i-Bahi, Harītī is shown holding cornucopia with her spouse Pāñchika holding a money bag in his hand[53].

Generally, the representation of a goddess carrying a child in her arms on the lap belongs to the *mātṛika* group. The Pāñcarakṣa goddess with *mātṛikas* are frequently referred to as *Skandamatas* with the epithet Durgā[54]. They were worshipped for the safety of pregnant women, during the period of pregnancy and gestation, safe delivery of the child and for the overall care and protection of the child, after the delivery. The worship of Pāñcarakṣa goddess with *mātṛikas* in Hindu pantheon reflects the influence of the Buddhist Pāñcarakṣa goddess. Probably during the medieval period, she was introduced into the Hindu pantheon as Yogēśvari (Protector of Children) as the eighth *mātṛika*.

Interestingly, several stone sculptures and plaques of fertility deity (nude Mother Goddess) are recovered both from the Buddhist and Brāhmanical sites. The goddess is also considered as the bestower of children by the Hindus. The tradition of worshipping the nude mother goddess (*Lajjagauri*) by the childless women continued as a living practice as evidenced in the Balabrahmesvara temple complex at Alampur in Mahabubnagar District. The discovery of such plaques from Buddhist sites such as Nagarjunakonda, Karlapalem and Gopalapatnam belonging to the early centuries of Christian era, and also from Brāhmanical temples at Alampur, Sangameswaram, Vellala, and Prathakota datable to the early medieval period suggests that the worship of the goddess was initiated by the Buddhists and later on borrowed by the Hindus. Basing on identical iconographical features she came to be identified with the Goddess Harītī. The early Chalukyas who ruled over Krishna-Tungabhadra valley styled themselves in inscriptions as *Harītī putras* (Sons of the goddess Harītī). In the present state of knowledge, it is difficult to identify the nude Mother Goddess (*Lajjagauri*) with Harītī, though both discharge similar function i.e. bestower of children or protector of children. Harītī as a Yakṣiṇi and giver of wealth is associated with the Yakṣa king Kubera, the lord of wealth as his spouse. She is a popular deity in Nepal, Tibet, China and Java. Several sculptures of this deity were reported from North Indian sites.

**Gaṇapati** : An interesting tāṅtric sculpture of standing Gaṇapati was carved on a boulder near the cave-entrance in Sankaram. Here, the lintel portion and facade of the cave are neatly dressed and carved with a *stūpa* motif in low relief. On the left side of the entrance is found a unique sculpture i.e. the tāṅtric form of Gaṇapati. He is represented with four hands standing in *samapāda* attitude. He holds a trident (*triśūl*) in the upper left hand, while his lower left carries a bowl (skull cup) and a severed human head. The object in the upper right hand is *ḍamaru* (not clearly visible) and in the lower right hand is a long sword with its edge pointed downwards. He is completely nude devoid of any drapery. He wears a long *kapāla māla* as *yajñōpavīta*. He is decked with armlets, bracelets and *kaṇṭhahāra*. His trunk is short and turned towards right (Pl. 8). Due to weathering, other iconographical features are not visible. On stylistic grounds, the sculpture may be assigned to 7th-8th c. A.D.

Towards left of the above sculpture, is another image portrayed with terrific features. He is represented with two hands holding a long sword and a severed human head, his feet trampling a *Prēta* (human corpse) which probably represents the trantric form of Heruka[55].

In the *Sādhanamāla,* only one *Sādhana* describes the form of Gaṇapati.[56]

*Bhagavantam Gaṇapatīṁ raktavarṇaṁ Jaṭāmakuṭa Kirīṭināṁ Sarvābharaṇa-bhāṣitam dvādaśabhujaṁ laṁbōdaraikavadanaṁ ardhaparyaṅka tāṇḍavaṁ trinētraṁ api ēkadantān savyabhujēṣu kuṭhāra-śara aṅkuśa-vajra-khaḍga-śūlāñca; vāmabhu-jēṣu mūsala-cāpa khaṭvāṅga asṛkkapāla phaṭkāñca rakta padmē mūṣikopari sthitam iti.*

'Gaṇapati is of red colour bearing the *jaṭāmakuṭa* decked in all ornaments having twelve arms, a protruding belly and one face. He stands in *ardhaparyaṅka* in dancing attitude. He is three eyed and has one tusk. He carries in his right hands the *kuṭhāra*, the arrow, the goad, the *vajra*, the sword and the *śūla* and in his left the *musala*, the bow, the *khaṭvāṅga*, the *kapāla* filled with blood, the *kapāla* with dried meat and the *phataka*. He rides the mouse on a red lotus'.

In the *Niṣpannayōgāvaḷi* he is described several times. In the *maṇḍala* of *Dharmadhātuvāgīśvara,* he is described as follows :

*Mūṣakē Gaṇapati Sitāh Karivaktraḥ Sarpayajñōpavīti Caturbhujaḥ savyābhyaṁ triśūla laḍḍukau vāmābhyaṁ paraśumūlake dadhana.*

'Gaṇapati is white complexioned and rides on a mouse. He is with an elephant face and wears a snake as his sacred thread. He is four armed. The two right hands hold the trident and the *laḍḍuka* (sweet ball) while the two left hands hold the *paraśu* (axe) and the *Mulaka* (radish)'[57]. In the *Bhūtadāmaramaṇḍala*, he is shown carrying *mulaka* and *paraśu* in the two right hands and *triśūla* and *kapāla* in the two left[58]. The sculpture of Gaṇapati under study tallies with the representation mentioned in the *Bhūtadāmaramaṇḍala* of *Niṣpannayōgāvaḷi*. It is a unique sculpture reported from South India.

An early representation of the figure Gaṇapati is found on the coping stone of Amaravati belonging to 1st-2nd c. A.D. The elephant-headed *yakṣa* type depicted on the coping stone is the earliest known representation of *Yakṣarāja* looking more like *Guhya-Gaṇa*[59]. He is shown prominently with elephant ears, short stumpy limphs, prominent pouch and stylised trunk curved towards right. The tusk is inconspicuous. The figure wears loin cloth, the tassels of which hang between the hips. He is decked in simple ornaments. In Vajrayāna, an attempt was made by the Buddhists to show the superiority of their gods over those of the Hindu gods. In Hindu pantheon, Gaṇēśa is considered as '*Siddhidāta*' or 'Bestower of perfection or success' and as a God, he occupied the foremost position among the Hindu gods, whereas the Vajrayānists, assigned the lowest position for Gaṇapati in their pantheon. For example, the icons such as Parṇasabari, Aparājita and Vighnāntaka etc., in Indian Museum and Baroda Museum are portrayed in such a way that Gaṇēśa was trampled by the Buddhist deities. The images like Parṇasabari and Mahā Paripratisara from Vikrampur, show Gaṇēśa as lying prostrate on the ground, crushed under the weight of Buddhist deities[60]. It shows the animosity or aversion towards Hindu gods of the Vajrayāna Buddhists in later times. Some times he is also shown in the company of Mañjuśrī and the Hindu God Viṣṇu (Bronze Icon. National Museum).

## NAGARJUNAKONDA

The famous Buddhist centre, Nagarjunakonda is situated about 20 kms. from Macherla in Guntur district. The site is named after the great Buddhist Teacher *Āchārya* Nagarjuna, the propounder of *Mādhyamika* school of Philosophy, who spent his last days in a monastery on the Śrīparvata hill. In inscriptions, Nagarjunakonda is referred to as *Śrīparvata*. There are no references to Nagarjunakonda, either in epigraphs or literature, till 16th century A.D. A lithic record of the king Vīra Purushadatta of Ikṣvāku dynasty call him as *Śrīparvatādhipati* whose capital city was Vijayapuri[61].

The discovery of coins belonging to Gautamīputra Satakarni, Vāsishṭhiputra Pulumāvi and Yajna Śrī Satakarni and an epigraph of the king Gautamiputra Vijaya Satakarni, dated in his 6th regnal year, clearly attest to the hold of the Sātavāhanas over the valley, before the Ikṣvākus[62]. The valley came into prominence only after the victory and annexation of some parts of the valley from the Sātavāhanas by Vāsishṭhiputra Chantamūla, founder of the Ikṣvāku dynasty. Other important members of the dynasty were, Madhariputra Vīrapurushadatta, Vāsishṭhiputra Ehavula Chantamūla and Vāsishṭhiputra Rudra Purushadatta. The kings and their queens, lay-worshippers and a number of monks from different parts of the country and also from distant lands like Ceylon have contributed their mite for the development of the Buddhist establishments at Nagarjunakonda, which made the valley a great centre of Buddhist learning. Each monastery was named after a sect, such as *Mahisāsaka, Bahusrutīya, Aparamahāvinasēlīya* etc. A Simhala *vihāra* probably meant exclusively for the monks from Ceylon was a prominent edifice. Thus, Nagarjunakonda or Vijayapuri became a prominent centre for the Buddhist monks, within a period of 200 years.

Excavations conducted at different places in the valley, brought to light a number of structures belonging to both Brāhmanical and Buddhist faiths of 3rd-4th centuries A.D. They comprise of *stūpas*, apsidal shrines and *vihāras*, such as Dharaṇi-*vihāra*, Kumara Nandi *vihāra*, Mahiśāsaka *vihāra*, Bahusrutīya *vihāra* etc. besides other structures like temples of Nodagīśvara, Kārtikeya and *aśvamēdha* complex. The secular structures include the arena, bathing ghat, residential structures and also structures relating to defence and military.

The above evidences such as coins, epigraphs and religious edifices facilitate to date the monastic complex of Nagarjunakonda to 3rd-4th c. A.D. The recently discovered copper plates of Pṛithivī Śrī Mūla Rāja, issued from Kondavidu, belonging to 5th-6th c. A.D. refer to a *Navakammika*, resident of Aparaśaila *vihāra*, who was appointed for the renovation works of the *Mahāvihāra* at Gunapasapura, identifiable with Taduru in Guntur district. Scholars have already identified the Aparaśaila *vihāra* mentioned in the inscriptions with Nagarjunakonda. From this, it becomes clear that the monastic complex at Nagarjunakonda continued to flourish as a prominent Buddhist centre upto the 6th century A.D[63].

Scholars are of the opinion that the Vajrayāna Buddhism had its origin in the valley of Nagarjunakonda under the leadership of one Nagarjuna. But there are no clear archaeological or literary evidences to confirm the fact except for few sculptural remains like the seated image of Harītī.

**Harītī** : Excavations at Nagarjunakonda brought to light, a mutilated image of Harītī, carved in lime stone, datable to Ikṣvāku times in the precincts of a brick temple with a pillared *maṇḍapa* in front, which was constructed to house the image for worship. The Goddess is shown seated with her legs dangling (Pl. 9). The girdle, the wristlets and the anklets are extant[64]. The discovery of a huge quantity of shell bangles obviously suggests that it was attracted a large number of nuns and lay women. Associated with the image were the early historic materials and a broken inscription in Brāhmi Characters. The inscription refers to a grant meant for setting up a perpetual lamp called *Akṣayanivi* on some special occasion or some important festival and also for its maintenance. The inscription reads as follows :[65]

*(cha) Tethika (na) ............... naka ...................*
*......... Lasa cha Bhadaphula Sathapa (sama) gandaka Vatava ki .........*
*bhujitavasa akhaya-nivikā datā gama .......pa.........*
*......... ham (ka) Koluram netachava (sam) ...........*
*.......... ya cha Apara (ma) ...........*
*...............sa cha (a Khaya) .... niv(i) d(i) iari māsakā (nam) divadham satam (bha) ...........*
*............Supayutam [1] esā cha akhayanivi ku(Li) ka ..... Pamukhāyam ............*
*........... atateya chi ......... yano (hi) ................*

Though the worship of Harītī as a goddess is found in early Buddhist literature, however it came into practice only at a later stage of the Mahāyāna phase. Several terracotta figurines of mother and child, either sitting or standing were reported from Buddhist sites in Āndhradēśa. Probably these figures stand as symbolic representations of the goddess Harītī. The occurrence of such figurines in terracotta suggests the popularity of the Goddess among common people during the early centuries of Christian era.

Interestingly, the early medieval inscriptions of Badami Chalukyas who ruled over Āndhradēśa between 6th and 9th centuries A.D. which includes some parts of Krishna-Tungabhadra valley, styled themselves as *Harītīputras*[66], i.e. sons of the goddess Harītī. But in this region, no such figures were reported. However, several sculptures of *Lajjagauri* (the nude Mother Goddess) known as the bestower or protector of children) belonging to the early Chalukyan period are available in this region. Hence, it is difficult to suggest whether the early Chalukyans worshipped the goddess Harītī as *Lajjagauri* which is iconographically different from Harītī though mythologically they are one and the same. A well preserved image of Harītī in stone and bronze came to light from Sankaram[67] and Dhulikatta[68] respectively in Andhra Pradesh.

## AMARAVATI

The world renowned Buddhist centre at Dhānyakaṭaka, presently known as Amaravati, is situated on the right bank of the river Krishna, about 35 kms. from Guntur. In ancient times, it was known as *Deepāladinne* (mound of lamps). The well fortified town 'Dharaṇikōṭa' which flourished as the capital city of the Sātavāhanas, lies 1 km. away from the present Amareswara temple complex.

It was an important inland port town during the pre-Christian era, through which, high class glass ornaments were imported from the Mediterranean region. The maritime trade activity at this site, during the early centuries of Christian era is also well attested by the occurrence of rouletted and arretine wares, Roman amphorae, and a good number of Roman coins[69].

The earliest reference to Amaravati occurs in a Prakrit inscription which calls it as *'Danakaḍa'*. Subsequent Sanskrit and Telugu inscriptions call it as Dhānyakaṭaka[70], Dhānyavāṭika, Dhānyaṁkapuraṁ, Dharaṇikōṭa, Dannālakōṭa, Dhannāḍa[71] etc. Hieun Tsang (640 A.D.), the Chinese traveller who visited this place when Buddhism was on the wane called it as 'Te-na-ka-che-ka', a Chinese version of 'Dhānyakaṭaka'[72].

Medieval inscriptions mention 'Dhānyakaṭaka' as a famous Buddhist centre, where Saivism also flourished since at least 10th century A.D. Interestingly, both the religions flourished together at this site for more than five centuries. A pillar inscription dated Circa 1100 A.D. records the visit of the Pallava king Simhavarman to '*Parama* Buddha *Kṣētra* of Dhānyakaṭaka'[73]. Another pillar epigraph from the same temple dated 1182 A.D., belonging to the reign of Kota Keta II, describes the architectural and sculptural embellishment of the *Mahāchaitya*, as *Chaityaṁ atyunnataṁ yatra nānā-chitra-Suchitritaṁ'*. Further, it also records certain endowments made by the king to the Lord Buddha[74]. Another record issued by Bayyamamba, wife of Kota Beta II dated 1234 A.D. refers to the offering of a perpetual lamp to the God Buddha at 'Śrī Dhanyaghati'[75]. From this, it is clear that the kings of medieval Āndhradēśa, though they were staunch followers of Saivism, patronised Buddhism liberally.

Further, it is interesting to learn that an inscription at Gadaladeniya in Kandy district, Ceylon, dated 1344 A.D.[76], perhaps the latest record, refers to certain restoration and renovation works done by Dharmakirti, a Sṭhavīra of Ceylon, to a two-storeyed image-house at Dhānyakaṭaka. This fact is also recorded in *Saddharma Ratnakāra,* a Ceylonese work of late medieval times, written by Vimalakīrti. There are no epigraphical or literary references to the place 'Dhānyakaṭaka' as a Buddhist centre after 15th century A.D.

As regards literature, the tāṅtric work *Sēkōddēśatīka* of medieval times refers to it as 'Śrīdhanya'. The *Mañjuśrī Mūlataṅtra*[77] refers to it as 'Śrīdhānyakaṭaka'. Some Tibetan works also mention the name as 'Siristhana i.e. Dhānyakaṭaka. The name 'Dharaṇikōṭa' appears to have been derived from *Dhārṇis* or *Maṅtras* (hymns)[78].

The earliest reference to the temple of 'Amareswara' at Amaravati occurs in an Eastern Chalukyan record of the king Chalukya Bheema, of 10th century A.D.[79]

This marks the ascendancy of Saivism and the gradual decline of Buddhism at Dhānyakaṭaka.

Excavations at the habitation site revealed five distinct cultural periods. In period V (6th-11th centuries A.D.) were found images of Vajrayāna, clay sealings with Buddhist creed formulae and other medieval cultural materials[80]. Thus, on the whole, the excavations carried out at different times and the occurrence of label epigraphs at the site, inform us clearly that Dhānyakaṭaka flourished as a prominent Buddhist centre since at least 4th-3rd centuries B.C. to 14th century A.D.

The occurrence of stone and bronze icons of Maitrēya, Mañjuśrī, Lokēśwara, Vajrapāṇi, Heruka etc. and clay tablets inscribed with Buddhist creed formulae of Vajrayāna faith clearly attest the gradual transformation of Mahāyāna Buddhism at Amaravati into its final Tāntric Vajrayāna form. The following Icons and images recorded at Dharanikota are taken up for study to correlate the iconographical features of the images with the *sādhanās* mentioned in the *Sādhanamāla*.

**Bronze Icons :** Altogether four bronzes belonging to Vajrayāna phase were unearthed in the excavations, of which three are highly mutilated and the other one is found intact[81]. All bronzes are hollow in nature and datable to 6th c. A.D. The standing Buddha icons show either the right hand in *varada* or *abhaya* mudrā while the left hand invariably holds the stalk of a flower (Pl. 10). Some scholars identified the object held in the left hand as the folds of his upper robe. On close observation, it is found to be the stem of a flower. Similar examples were reported from Nelakondapalli[82], Buddham[83] and Gummadidurru[84]. However these bronzes are the earliest forms of Bōdhisattva Avalōkitēśvara or Padmapāṇi so far encountered in Āndhradēśa. Only two icons are selected for study.

**(i) Avalōkitēśvara :** Standing *Bōdhisattva* (43.5 cm.) which is intact shows the right hand in *varada mudrā* while the left hand holds the stalk of a flower. The mark of *Uṛna* is absent. *Uṣṇīṣa* shows protruberance covered by curls of hair and shaped like a conical cap. It is entirely different from the other specimens especially in the depiction of *Uṣṇīṣa*, facial features and other icnographical features.

**(ii) Padmapāṇi or Avalōkitēśvara :** Though slightly mutilated, it exhibits indigeneous traits particularly in the depiction of *Uṣṇīṣa* and facial features. The icon (28.5 cm. high) has no *Uṛna* mark. The right hand is either in *abhaya mudrā* or *bhūmisparśa mudrā* while the left hand holds the stalk of a flower. The *Uṣṇīṣa* is prominently shown covered with small globular curls made into a round bun (Pl. 11).

**Sculptures :** Several stone images were reported through explorations and excavations conducted in and around the village. Images carved in lime stone and other granite materials range chronologically from 7th c.-8th c. A.D. to 9th c.-10th c. A.D.

**Buddha in *Bhūsparśa Mudrā* (Akṣobhya)** : The lime stone image (17" × 9" × 2") of Buddha depicted in *vajraparyaṅkāsana* (adamantine sitting) attitude, seated on lotus pedestal is depicted with two hands. His right hand is shown in *Bhūmisparśa mudrā* while his left hand is kept on the lap (Pl. 12). In this posture, except for the thumb, all the tips of the four fingers of the right palm are drawn inwardly and shown touching the earth as if the Master himself was calling the mother earth to witness his victory over Mara and also his attainment of the Supreme Knowledge. Several sculptures of *Dhyāni* Buddha Akṣobhya are also available in the same attitude, but these can be distinguished only on the basis of colour variation of the images.

Here, the depiction of a standing figure with offerings on the pedestal suggests the symbolic representation of the mother earth who emerged out to witness the spiritual powers of the Master. The *dhyāna* given in the *Sādhanamāla* for his worship is as follows :[85]

*Savyakarena Bhūsparśa mudrāṁ ut sangasthit vasavyahastaṁ kāsāyavastra vagunthanam nilagauraraktaśyamacatur-maropari-Viśva padmavajravasthitam Śāntam laksanavyan-janenavitāgatram Jaṭamakuṭinam Savyakarena cāmara-ratnadhāriṇaṁ avasavyēna Nāgakēśara-puṣpacchata dhāram. Tathā vāmato Lōkēśvarraṁ Śukla dakṣina karena cāmaradharaṁ vāmakarena kamalādharaṁ Bhagavanmukhā vlōkanaparu catau bhāvayet. Iti Vajrāsana sādhanaṁ samā ptam.*

'He sits on the *vajra* marked with double lotus in *vajrapāryaṅkāsana* in *Bhūsparśa mudrā*. He is peaceful in appearance and his body is endowed with all the major and minor auspicious marks. He is dressed in red garments. To the right of the God is Maitrēya Bōdhisattva holding chowry jewel and the *Nāgakēśara* flower in his hands.' The *Pāñcakara* section of the *Advayavajra saṅgraha* describes him as follows :[86]

*Sūryamaṇḍalastha-nila-Hūṁkaraniṣpanno dvibhuya ekamukho Bhūsparśa-mudrādharo Vajraparyaṅki............ Vijñānaskandhasvabhā vah............. Vajrakuli ............. śiśiramadhyāhnaka tuśruti-akaśaśabada-cavargo Akṣobhya-Viśuddah*

'Akṣobhya originates from the blue syllable Hūṁ which is placed on the orb of the Sun. He is two armed and one faced, exhibits the *Bhūsparśa* (earth touching) *mudrā* and sits in the *vajraparyaṅkāsana* (adamantine) pose. He represents the primordial cosmic element of Vijñāna (consciousness). He is the embodiment of Vajra family and represents the winter season, noon-time, pungent taste, faculty of hearing, the element of Ether and sound and the Ca (palata) group of letters.' In the *Niṣpannayōgāvaḷi,* he is described as follows :[87]

*Akṣobhyah Kṛṣṇo raudraḥ Sitaraktasavyetaramukhah Savyakaraiḥ Kulacakra Padmāni Vāmir-ghaṇṭā-Cintāmaṇi-Khaḍgāṅ Vibhrāṇaḥ Svābha sparśa Vājrālingitaḥ.*

'Akṣobhya is blue in colour and is angry looking. The colour of his right face is white and that of the left is red. He holds in his right hands the *vajra,* the disc and the lotus. In the three left hands he carries the bell, the *cintāmaṇi* jewel and the sword. With the two principal hands he embraces the Prajñā sparśavajra by name.'

Gautama, (Śākyasiṁha) the last of group of the seven mortal Buddhas is frequently depicted both in sculpture and paintings. In *Bhūsparśa mudrā* he is shown endowed with the thirty-two major and eighty minor auspicious marks, three kinds of mental characteristics (i.e. the ten *balas* or forces, eighteen *Avenika dhārṇas* or peculiar properties and the four *vaisaradyas* or points of self-confidence or assurance). In paintings, he is shown in yellow or gold colour. Generally, on the pedestal are found an elephant, horse or the corpulent squatting swords-man, damsel with folded arms, *cakra*, the financier, squatting bearded man with skulls, some offerings etc.[88]

The sculptures of this type are found commonly in north Indian sites such as Saranath, Patna and in the Indian Museum. In Andhra, they were reported from Salihundam and Sankaram. Interestingly a terracotta plaque depicting Buddha in *Bhūsparśa mudrā* is reported from Sabhar[89]. The Hinayāna Buddhists in Java, Ceylon, Burma and Siam worship Gauthama Buddha in the form of Akṣobhya[90].

**Maitrēya***:* Of the two lime-stone images discovered at the site, one is shown represented (12" × 11" × 2½") with two hands and seated in *pratyalīdha* attitude on a decorated throne. It is in good state of preservation. His right hand is in *varada mudrā,* while the left hand holds a *Nāgakēśara* flower. The right leg is folded and the left leg is kept akimbo resting on a lotus *pīṭha* or seat. He is heavily ornamented with bracelets, prominent necklaces, armlets and an elaborate head-gear. The lower garment is depicted very meticulously and tied by means of *mēkhala*. On the left corner of the pedestal, below the folded leg, is a male figure in kneeling posture with upraised hands in *añjali* attitude (Pl. 13). There is a *chaitya* motif prominently seen behind the throne by which he can be distinguished from the figure of Padmapāṇi. The inscription on the grey colour lime stone image reads[91]

*"ye dharma hetu Prabha*
*Tathāgato hyava..............*
*(Tesan) chayē*
*nirōdhō ēyamva*
*di mahā Sramanah"*

It means 'Tathāgata has revealed the cause of phenomena which spring from a cause and also their cessation. So says the monk.'

According to the Buddhist literature, he is a mortal Bōdhisattva supposed to be waiting in Tusita heaven to come down to the earth in human form as a future Buddha. He was to come to the earth 4000 years after the disappearance of Buddha for the deliverance of all sentient beings. He is honoured by both Hinayānists and Mahāyanists. The *Sādhana* provides the following *Dhyāna* for his worship as follows[92]:

..........*Pita 'Maim kara parinataṁ viśvakamalasthitaṁ trimukhaṁ caturbhujaṁ kṛṣṇaśukla dakkṣiṇavāmamukhaṁ suvarṇagauraṁ Sattava paryaṅkinaṁ Vyākhya-namudrā-dharakaradvyaṁ aparadaksināvama bhujabhyāṁ varada puṣpita nāga-kēśara mañjari dharaṁ nānā lankāradharam ātmānaṁ Maitrēyarūpam aiambya Maitrēyasādhanam.*

'He is three faced, three eyed and four armed. His right and left faces are of blue and white colour respectively. He is in yellow colour. He sits in the *paryaṅka* attitude on animal and his two hands are in *vyākhyāna mudrā* and his right hand is in *varada mudrā* while the left hand holds *Nāgakēśara* flower.'

In the *Mañju vajra Maṇḍala* of *Niṣpannayōgāvaḷi*[93] he iṣ described as "*Maitrēyaḥ Suvarṇavarṇo dvābhyāṁ Kṛtadharmadeśanāmudro varadasavyakaro vāmēna sapuśpanāga keśara pallavadharaḥ*".

'He is in golden colour represented with two principal hands in *dharmachakra mudrā* and the lower right hand in *varada mudrā* while the lower left hand holds the twig of the *Nāgakēśara* flower.'

In the *Durgatipariśodhana maṇḍala* of *Niṣpannayōgāvaḷi*[94], he is described as *'Maitrēyah Pītam Savyakarena Nāgakēśarakusumaṁ vāmēna kundīṁ dadhānah'.*

'He is of golden colour. The right hand holds the flower of *Nāgakēśara* and the left hand a mendicant bowl.'

In the *Sādhanamāla*[95], he is described as *Maitrēyaḥ pitavarnaścanāga-puṣpavarapradaḥ* 'Maitrēya is in yellow colour and holds the *Nāgakēśara* flower in his left hand and the right hand is in *varada mudrā*.'

Getty says that in the Indian sculptures Maitrēya is shown seated as a Buddha with legs interlocked or dangling down. Ṣometimes he bears figures of the five

*Dhyāni* Buddhas on the *prabhāvaḷi* of the image. Invariably a *chaitya* motif is seen in the head-gear. He is shown in *Dharmacakra mudrā* with a vase and wheel supported by the stems of *Nāgakēśara* flowers. He is also represented both in standing and sitting attitudes. He heads the list of Bodhisattavas in the *Niṣpannayōgāvaḷi*. He takes the form of spiritual sires Vairocana and Akṣobhya. The inscription at Turfan in Central Asia refers to a temple dedicated to Maitrēya in 469 A.D.[96] The earliest sculpture in India is reported from Gāndhāra school of art. The cult was popular only from 5th-6th centuries A.D. onwards. Hieun-Tsang mentions the existence of Maitrēya in Udyana (U-chang-na). He further says that a sculpture in wood nearly 150 ft. high was worshipped at Dardu in the north-province of Punjab.[97] There are a number of sculptures in Borbodur temple in Java datable to 8th-9th centuries A.D.

**Buddha and Padmapāṇi :** It is also a lime stone panel (17"×9"×2") depicting the figures of (a) Buddha and (b) Padmapāṇi.

**(a) Buddha (Akṣobhya) :** He is seated in *Vajraparyaṅka* attitude. The depiction of *vajra* at the centre suggests the symbolical representation of Buddha in *vajrāsana*. His right hand is in *Bhūsparśa mudrā,* while the left hand is kept on the lap. He has a conical *Uṣṇīṣa* and pierced earlobes. The prominent drapery and halo besides acute iconographical features of the face obviously suggest the meticulous care taken by the sculptor in the delineation of the panel.

**(b) Padmapāṇi :** He is seated in *pratyalīdha* attitude. Of the two hands, the right one is in *varada mudrā* while the left hand is in *vitarka mudrā* holding the stem of a lotus. There is another lotus flower on the other side. He has an elaborately decorated crown, ear lobes and a necklace. A devotee is depicted on the pedestal.

The Bōdhisattva Padmapāṇi, the non-tāṅtric form of Avalōkitēśvara, is the spiritual emanation of the *Dhyāni* Buddha Amitābha. It is said that after the Nirvāṇa of the Buddha, Padmapāṇi is supposed to have undertaken the process of propagation of Buddhism until the creation of the fifth world by *Viśvapāṇi*. He is a popular deity in Tibet and Japan. In Ceylon and South East Asian countries, he is shown sitting in *rājalilāsana* attitude, keeping his right hand in *vitarka*, *abhaya or varada mudrās* and his left hand holds a full blown lotus flower[98]. He is represented with lotus symbol and some times a vase is also shown in support. A beautiful gold plated bronze image of Maitrēya is reported from Melaiyur (Tanjavur district) and also at Nagapattanam in Tamilnadu[99].

**Jñāna Visudha Heruka :** This is the earliest image reported from South India. The lime stone sculpture (10"×7"×3") portrays Heruka in *ardhaparyaṅka* pose keeping the sole of right foot touching the ankle of the left leg and shown with two hands. He holds the *vajra* in his right hand and the *kapāla* in his left. The *khaṭvāṅga* hangs down from his left shoulder. He wears *kuṇḍalas*, necklace of bones sewed by guts, *yajñōpavīta*, *prakōṣṭhavalayas* and *mēkhala*. The lower garment that extends upto the ankles is secured by *mēkhala*. His hair rises upwards and forms into a crown (Pl. 15).

In *Hēvajra Sādhana tantra*[100], he is described as, *Ēkamukham Jñānavisuddham dvibhujaṁ Śūnyatakaruṇa visuddhaṁ, dakṣiṇatho vajramabhēdya jñāna pratipādakam, Vamē kapāla khaṭvāṅgaṁ cha khaṭvāṅgaṁ Prajñāshva bhavarūpam, kapālam, bōdhichitta pradipadākam.*

'He is one faced and two armed. He holds the *vajra* in his right hand and the *kapāla* in his left. The *khaṭvāṅga* hangs from his left shoulder.

'Here, the *vajra* symbolises *abhēdya jñāna* or the knowledge of oneness in every thing. The *khaṭvāṅga* symbolises *Prajñā* or the highest knowledge and the *kapāla* stands for the *Bodhicitta* or the will to enlightenment. He is represented singly or with his consort with one or three faces. Among the emanations of *Dhyāni* Buddha Akṣobhya, Heruka stands pre-eminent. The yab-yum form of Heruka and Hēvajra are the chief gods in the family of Akṣobhya.'

When represented alone, he is depicted as standing on a corpse or in the prostrate form of Bhairava with his consort Kālarātri in either *alīdha* or the *pratyalīdha* attitude or dances in *ardha paryaṅka* attitude (Pl. 15a). In the *Sādhanamāla* the dhyāna for his worship in verse is as follows[101]:

*Śavasthaṁ ardhaparyaṅkaṁ naracarmasuvāsasaṁ*
*Bhasmoddhūlitagātrañca sphuradvajrañca daksinaṁ*
*Calatpatākākhaṭvāṅgaṁ vāme raktarotakaṁ*
*Śatārdhamundamālābhihkṛta hāramanoramaṁ*
*Iṣaddaṁṣṭrākarālāsyaṁ raktanetraṁ vilāsinaṁ*
*Piṅgorddhvakeśaṁ Akṣobhyamukutaṁ karnakuṇḍalaṁ*
*Asthyābharanaśobham tu śirah pañcakapālakaṁ*
*Buddhatvadāyinaṁ dhyāyāti Jagānmaranivāranaṁ.*

'Heruka standing on a corpse in *ardhaparyaṅka* attitude carries a *kapāla,* filled with blood in his left hand, while his right hand carries a *khaṭvāṅga* with a flowing banner like a sacred thread. He is well clad in human skin which is smeared with ashes. His face is shown with bare fangs and blood-shed eyes. He wears a necklace of about fifty severed heads. His hair drawn into a conical head-gear, bears the effigy of Akṣobhya. He wears *kuṇḍala* and other ornaments made out of bones. His head is beautified by five skulls. He bestows Buddha-hood and protects the world from the Maras. He stands on his left leg, over a double lotus, while placing the one on his left thigh in a dancing attitude. The *khaṭvāṅga* is marked with a *vajra* of five prongs and decorated with bells, human heads and double lotus. He wears a necklace of human heads.'

In the Hēvajra Maṇḍala of *Niṣpannayōgāvaḷi*, Heruka is the main deity when is accompanied by his *prajñā* and so he is known as Hēvajra. A separate Taṅtra called *Heruka Taṅtra* is exclusively devoted to his worship. A beautiful image which corresponds to the textual description of *Sādhanamāla* is reported from Dacca Museum[102]. He is invoked as bestowing the Buddhahood and as a protector against all the wordly evils.

He is popular in Tibet. As Hēvajra, he is also known as Trailōkyakṣēpa, Vajravarāhi, Buddha kapāla, Saṁbāra, Saptākṣara, Mahāmāya[103] etc. Heruka or Hēvajra is worshipped commonly in Nepal and Tibet.

**Sugati Sandarśana Lōkēśvara** : This standing image with four hands, holds a rosary in his upper right hand, while keeping the other in *abhaya mudrā,* in the upper left hand is a *kamaṇḍala* (water pot) while the lower left hands is in akimbo Posture (Pl. 16). The *Dhyāna Maṅtra* for the image is :[104]

*Sugati sandarśana-Lōkēśvara-Bhaṭṭārakam śuklavarnaṁ sadbhujaṁ varadābhayākṣamālā dharaṁ dakṣiṇe, vāme padmakundītri dandīdharaṁ ca ratnābharanabhūṣitaṁ vratasūtradhārinaṁ jaṭāmakuṭaṁ padmoparicandramaṇḍala-sthitaṁ saumyarūpaṁ bhāvayet*

'He is white in complexion having six hands. The three on the right are shown in *varada* and *abhaya mudrās* and a rosary respectively while the hands on the left carry the lotus, the water pot and the staff with three horns respectively. He is decorated with ornaments exhibiting the sacred thread prominently. He has a matted hair drawn into a crown. He stands on the moon over a lotus and appears peaceful.'

Among the fifteen important forms of Avalōkitēśvara, Sugati Śandarśana Lōkēśvara occupies a prominent place.

**Khadiravanī Tārā (Syāmatārā) :** Two images of the diety were reported from this site. A limestone image (17"×12"×4") represented with two hands and sitting on a lotus throne in *lalitāsana*, is broken and the head missing. Her right leg is kept in akimbo while the left leg rests on a lotus *pīṭha* or pedestal. Her right hand is in *varada mudrā* touching the soil with palm drawn outwardly (*Bhūsparśa mudrā*) while the left hand holds half-blown blue lotus (*nīlōtpala*) in the *vitarka mudrā*. She is heavily decorated with jewellery. The folds of the lower garment are prominently shown (Pl. 17). A *Dhyāna* in *Sādhanamāla* describes her as :[105]

*Haritāṁ Amōghasiddhimakutīṁ Varado paladhāridaksinavāmkarāṁ Aśōkakantā-Mārīcy-Ēkajaṭā Vyāgra dakṣiṇavāmadig bhāgaṁ divyakumāriṁ dhyātva Khadiravaṇī Tārā-Sādhanam.*

'Khadrivaṇī Tārā is of green colour, bears the image of *Dhyāni* Buddha Amōgha Siddhi on her crown. Her right hand exhibits *varada mudrā,* while the left one holds *utpala*. To her right and left are *Aśōka kāntā Mārīcī* and *Ēkajaṭā*. She appears as celestial virgin.'

Here, though the representation of two attendant deities Aśōkakāntā, Mārīcī and Ēkajaṭā are conspicously absent, the other iconographical features correspond to the textual description given in the *Sādhanamāla*. The absence of these features suggests the early sculptural representation of the Goddess.

The name, Tārā is commonly applied to all the feminine deities in Buddhist pantheon. It is difficult to distinguish white or green. The Tārā under study is the emanation of Amōghasiddhi, otherwise also known as Syāma Tārā, the colour generally depicted is green[106]. As *Sādhana* does not mention the *āsana*, she might be represented either as standing or sitting (Pl. 17a).

Images reported from Tibet and China were noticed at Salihundam in A.P. The Tibetans considered the deity as the original Tārā and is familiarly known as *Dongon* (original Tārā) which symbolises the Divine energy. In Tibetan banners she is figured at the centre surrounded by twenty one Tārās, of which ten are white, five red and five yellow in colour[107].

b) The second image (8½" × 7"×3") is also similar to the above in all respects. It is an intact sculpture with all the iconographical features.

**Mahāchīnatārā or Ugra Tārā** : This standing lime stone image (13"×7"×3") in *pratyalīdha* pose is represented with four hands. She holds a sword and a knife in her two right hands, a black lotus and a skull in her two left hands. She wears a garland of skulls, besides heavily ornamented jewellery. Though the face is mutilated, the representation of third eye on the forehead is discernible. The lower garment worn by her may be tiger's skin. The terrible form of goddess with a short and sturdy body exhibiting prominent breasts, stands on a corpse (Pl. 18). She is one of the angry Goddesses, resembling the attributes of the Dharmapala form of the Gods. She is also known as Blue Tārā Ekajaṭā[108].

In Buddhist literature she is known as *Ugra Tārā*. She was incorporated into the Hindu pantheon as Tārā and worshiped as one of the ten *Mahāvidya* goddesses. There are two *Sādhanās* devoted to the worship of Ugra Tārā. In the *Sādhanamāla* (1165 A.D.) and also in *Śāśvata vajra,* the *Dhyāna* gives her form as follows :[109]

*Pratyālīdhapadāṁ ghorāṁ muṇḍamālāpralambitāṁ*
*Kharvalambodārāṁ bhīmāṁ nīlanīrājarajitāṁ*
*Tryambakaikamukhāṁ divyāṁ ghorāṭṭahāsabhāsurāṁ*
*Suprahṛṣtāṁ śavārūdhāṁ nāgāṣṭakavibhūsitāṁ*
*Raktavarttutanetrāñca vyāghracarmāvṛtāṁ kaṭau*
*Navayauvanasampannāṁ pañcamudrāvibhusitāṁ*
*Lalajjihvāṁ mahābhīmāṁ sadaṁṣṭrotkaṭabhīsanāṁ*
*Khaḍgakartrikarāṁ savye vāmotpalakapāladhāṁ*
*Pingograikajatāṁ dhyāyāt maulāv-Akṣobhyabhūṣitaṁ*
*Mahācīna-tārā-Sādhanaṁ.*

'Standing in the *pratyalīdha* posture, she wears a lengthy garland in the neck. She is short and has protruding belly and tongue. Her complexion is that of blue lotus. She is one faced, three eyed, laughs horribly standing on a corpse. She is decked with snakes as ornaments and the garments of tiger skin. Endowed with five auspicious symbols, she is terrible in appearance with bare canine fangs and carries a sword and *kartri* in the two right hands and *utpala* and the *kapāla* in her two left hands. Her *jaṭāmakuṭa* bears the image of Akṣobhya.'

The *Dhyāna* mentioned in *Mahācīna-Taṅtra* is the earliest one than the *Dhyāna* mentioned in *Sādhanamāla*. The Hindu Tāṅtric works like *Tārārahasya* of Brahmananda (16th c. A.D.) and the *Taṅtrasāra* of Krishnananda Āgamavāgīśa mention the *Dhyāna* which is more or less similar to the *Dhyāna* mentioned in the *Ṣaḍgabāṇaka*.[110]

*Pratyalīḍhapadaṁ ghorāṁ muṇḍamālāvibhūsitāṁ*
*Kharvaṁ lambodarīṁ bhīmāṁ vyāghracarmāvṛtāṁ kaṭau*
*Navayauvanasampannāṁ pañcamudrāvibhūsitāṁ*
*Chaturbhujām lolajihvāṁ mahābhīmaṁ varapradām*
*Khaḍgakartrisamāyuka-savyetarabhujadvayāṁ*
*Kapālotpalasaṁyuktasavyapāniyugānvitāṁ*
*Pingograikajaṭaṁ dhyāyenmaulāv Akṣobhyabhūṣitāṁ*
*Bālārkamaṇḍalākāralocanatrayabhūṣitāṁ*
*Jalaccitāmadhyagatāṁ ghoradaṁṣṭrāṁ karāliṇīṁ*
*Sāveśasmeravadanāṁ stryalaṅkāravibhūṣitāṁ*

*Viśvavyāpakatoyāntaḥ śvētapadmoparisthitāṁ*
*Akṣobhyadevīmūrdhanyastrimūrtirnāgarupadhṛk*

A remarkable difference found in the verses of *Taṅtrasāra* and *Sādhanamāla* is that the verse in the *Sādhanamāla* is substantially modified, grammatically corrected and rectified by the later Hindu tāṅtric authors.

Here, the goddess stands on the corpse. In the Hindu pantheon, she is *Śakti* consort to Mahādeva. The only difference of the Hindu deities is the absence of effigy of parental God from whom they emanated. She is the most powerful of all Goddesses. Repeated chanting of *maṅtras* for her worship, destroys all obstacles, confers good luck and intense religious enjoyment.

**Jambhāla** : A mutilated image of Jambhāla in stucco was unearthed near a brick built enclosure (129' × 62') away from the *Mahāchaitya*[111]. The exterior wall is embellished with a number of Tāṅtric sculptures in the niches. Within the enclosure was the shrine (14' × 14') dedicated to Jambhāla. The figure made in lime plaster is in uncouth corpulent sitting in squatting posture. The oval shaped lump at the chest and the folded right arm obviously suggest that he held a citron (*Jambhara*). His left palm is placed on the belly. A thick strap in between the chest and abdomen and the nave are shown very prominently (Pl. 19).

Of all the emanations of Akṣobhya, Jambhāla the god of wealth (Kubēra) is shown without terrible features. His parental *Dhyāni* Buddha is either Ratnasaṁbhava or Akṣobhya. Jambhāla emanating from Ratnasaṁbhava carries the mongoose in his right hand and citron in the left. The mongoose is supposed to be the receptacle of all gems and jewels. He distributes gems and riches to his devotees. The *Dhyāna* in the *Sādhanamāla* describes him as follows :[112]

*Jambhālaṁ trimukham ṣaḍbhujaṁ Akṣobhyajaṭāmukuṭinaṁ dakṣiṇatribhujah mātulungā-ṅkusa-bānadharaṁ-prathamvāmabhujaikena vama-pārśvasthita-Prajāliṅgitaṁ-aparavāmabhujābhyāṁ sapāśanakulī-kārmukadharaṁ ātmanāṁ niṣpādya.*

'He is represented with three faces and six arms. An effigy of Akṣobhya is on the head-gear. He carries a citron, a goad and an arrow in his right hands while with his left principal hand he embraces the *Prajñā* and carries a mongoose tied around with a lasso and an arrow.'

A miniature stone image of Jambhāla in Decca Museum contains a label inscription in Bengali script which reads *'Jambhāla Jalē (ndra) ya svāha'*. It means Jambhāla is not only identified with Kubēra but also with *Varuṇa* (the lord of waters).[113] Another example of Kubēra shows the God seated in crouching position holding a *kapāla* in the right hand while the left rests on the neck of a mongoose which hangs over the left knee. He is ornamented with serpents and in his head-dress is a small image of *Dhyāni* Buddha[114].

Jambhāla is a Yakṣa of non-Buddhist origin. He receives great respect from all the devotees. As a God of wealth, he has a separate entity and worshipped in all the Buddhist countries as attested by the evidence at Amaravati[115]. A unique bronze having three legs and five heads with the feet of legs on skulls and decorated with serpent ornaments is reported.[116] He is also represented in yab-yum form in golden yellow complexion in paintings. In this aspect, he has three faces and six arms. His two faces to the right and left are red and blue complexioned. He sits in *vajraparyaṅkāsana* and embraces his *prajñā* Vasudhara with his two principal hands. Jambhāla in another form shows two hands holding citron and mongoose in *ālīḍha* attitude and tramples upon two semi-divine beings *viz.* Śaṅkhamuṇḍa and Padmamuṇḍa[117].

Images of this form are reported from Gāndhāra, Saranath, Mathura, Magadha, Bengal, Nepal, Tibet and China. Jambhāla in *Lalitakśēpa* posture is reported from Nepal and Vikrampur. His terrible form known as ucchusma-Jambhāla is reported from Saranath only[118]. In Tibet, a special ceremony called 'yan yung' for imploring Kubera for riches, plays an important part in the Taṅtras, in sorcery and exorcism[119].

**Buddha with Maitrēya and Padmapāṇi :** It is an interesting lime stone panel (19½"×12"×2½") showing Buddha in the centre flanked by Maitrēya and Padmapāṇi. Buddha is shown in *Vajraparyaṅkāsana* with his right hand in *Bhūsparśa mudrā* while the left hand rests on the lap. Other iconographical features tally with those of other images reported earlier. To his right is a seated image of Maitrēya in *pratyalīdha* attitude, with his right leg kept resting on the *Pīṭha*. His left hand holds the Nāgakēśara flower while his right hand is in *vyākhyāna* mudrā. He has elaborate and decorated head-dress. He wears *kanaka kamālas, kēyūras* and *nūpuras*. To his left is a seated figure of Padmapāṇi in *pratyalīdha* pose. His right hand is placed on the right lap while the left hand holds the full blown lotus flower (Pl. 20).

**Padmapāṇi :** This is a standing Bōdhisattva in *tribhaṅga* pose with his left hand on the waist *(Kaṭihasta)* and his right hand holding stalk of a lotus (Pl. 21). He is decked with ornaments. He has a prominent head gear. A double *vajra* above the right shoulder suggests the tāṅtric aspect of Padmapāṇi. (It is displayed in London Museum).[120]

**Avalōkitēśvara :** Standing Bōdhisattva in *Samabhaṅga* attitude on a pedestal is holding the stalk of a lotus with his left hand and a vase or rosary in his right hand. He is well ornamented with jewels. He has a well decorated head-gear with an effigy of the figure *Dhyāni* Buddha Amitābha (Pl. 22). A pair of *Dhyāni* Buddhas i.e. Amitābha over the left and Akṣobhya over the right shoulder are depicted prominently. The features such as oval face, thick lips, snubbed nose and smiling face clearly suggest south Indian art tradition. The iconometrical details help us to date the sculpture to the Chalukyan times i.e. 8th-9th century A.D. (It is also in London Museum).[121]

**Padmapāṇi :** This image of standing Bōdhisattva is represented with two hands. The left hand is on the waist (*Katihasta*) whereas the other is broken and missing (Pl. 21a). The posture obviously indicates holding of the lotus flower with his right hand.[122] The drapery, ornaments and headgear suggest an early date i.e. 2nd-3rd centuries A.D. to the sculpture. Similar examples were reported from Nandayapalem[123] and Goli.[124]

**Buddha** (Akṣobhya) : He is seated in *Vajrāsana* with *bhūsparśa mudrā* (2'.5" height). *Trivali,* one of the *Mahapurusha lakshanas* is prominently seen on the neck. The features like elongated ear lobes, round face, closed eyes, *Urṇa* on the forehead, the halo behind the head etc. suggest the indegenous art of the early Chalukya or Pallava school. The facial features indicate a rare attitude of contemplation. (Pl. 23) The *Uṣṇiṣa* on the cranium is not very well developed like in the other images of medieval period reported from Tamil Nadu and south western part of Andhra Pradesh, which provides an early date i.e. 7th-8th c. A.D. for this image. (A. Aiyyappan : 1960)

**Siṁhanāda Avalōkitēśvara :** The two headed image of Siṁhanāda is shown seated in *Mahārāja lilāsana* on a couchant lion (3 ft. height). The right arm is in *chin-mudrā* while the left arm holds the stalk of a lotus, coming out of a vase supported by a double lotus which looks like a *damaru.* A sword above the full blown lotus indicates a cognisance of the deity. The hind part of *vāhana* is decorated with a string of bells. On the right side of the figure is a trident, the handle of which is entwined by a serpent. (Pl. 24) The representation of trident, the depiction of waist band in the shape of a bowl and also the other iconographical features obviously suggest the influence of the early Chalukyan or Pallava art. (A. Aiyyappan : 1960)

The depiction of *trivali* on the neck, the round face, neatly arranged *jaṭā makuṭa,* simple garments devoid of ornaments and other iconometric details clearly suggest early features for the image, datable to 7th-8th centuries A.D. The posture and facial features indicate majesty, added with great determination rather than spiritual contemplation. Four *sādhanas* are given for the worship of Simhanada which are alike in all respects. The *sādhana* mentioned in the *sādhanamāla* is as follows :

*Ātmānaṁ Siṁhanāda-Lokeśvararūpam bhāvayet, śvetavarnaṁ trinetraṁ jatāmukuṭinaṁ nirbhūṣanaṁ vyāghracarmaprābhṛtaṁ siṁhā-sanasthaṁ mahārājaliṁ candrāsanaṁ candraprabham bhāvayet. Dakṣiṇe sitaphaṇiveṣṭitaṁ triśūlaṁ śvetaṁ, vāme nānāsugandhikusuma-paripūritapadmabhājanaṁ. Vāmahastāt utthaṁ padmopari jvalatkhadgaṁ."*

"The worshipper should think of himself as Simhanāda Lokēśvara of white complexion,with three eyes, and the *jaṭāmakuṭa* (crown of matted hair). He is without ornaments, clad in tiger-skin, and seated on a lion in the attitude of princely ease. He is seated on the orb of the moon and is radiant like her. To his right, there is a white trident entwined by a white snake, and on the left there is a lotus-bowl full of fragrant flowers. From his left hand a lotus on which there is a sword burning like fire." (B. Bhattacharya : 1928)

The sculpture is more or less carved in accordance with the *Sādhana* or *dhyāna* mentioned in the texts, except in the depiction of ornaments, rosary and the bowl of flowers. Here, he is shown with a vase and a flower. There are no *yagñopavita* and rosary which are generally seen in other sculptures. In the absence of ornamentation, the image seems to be different from some of the forms of Mañjuśrī. It is an excellent and exquisitively carved specimen dated to 8th-9th c. A.D. Vajrayānists believe that his worship cured from all diseases. He is one of the popular forms of Avalōkitēśvara. Images of this type are reported from Mahoba, Nepal, Magadha, Tibet and China.

**Manñjughōsha :** The sculpture (3 ft. height) is carved on granite stone. He is seated in *sukhāsana* aspect on a lotus pedestal, keeping the right leg hanging down while the left is bent and placed on a pedestal. He wears a *karaṅḍa makuṭa* which looks like a conical cap with the figure of *dhyāni* Buddha Akṣobhya at its base. He is well decked with ornaments and jewellery. (A. Aiyyappan : 1960). The right hand is in *chin mudrā (Vyākhyāna mudrā)* whereas the left hand holds stalk of a lily flower. (Pl. 25). The facial and iconographical features indicate suggestiveness and serenity of the God which are the main features of Vajrayāna theology. The *Sādhana* mentioned in the *Sādhanamālā* is as follows :

*"Mañjughoṣarūpam-ātmānaṁ paśyet siṁhasthaṁ kanakagauravarnaṁ sarvā-*

*laṅkārabhūsitaṁ Vyākhyānamudrāvyagrakaraṁ vāmapārsve utpala-dharam Akṣ obhyamukuṭiṇam. Dakṣiṇe Sudhanakumāraṁ vāme Yamāntakaṁ paśyet....mantraṁ japet Oṁ Vāgīśvara Mūḥ."*

'The worshipper should meditate upon as the deity Mañjughōṣa who rides a lion, and is of golden yellow colour. He is decked in all ornaments, and his hands are engaged in forming the *vyākhyāna* (teaching) *mudrā*. He displays the night lotus in his left, and bears the image of Akṣobhya on his crown. On his right there is Sudhana-kumara and on the left Yamāntaka.... The *Mantra Oṁ Vāgīśvara Mūḥ'* should be muttered. (B. Bhattacharya : 1928)

Some of the *sādhanas* mention that he should sit in *lalitāsana* on the back of the lion whereas others prescribe *vajraparyaṅka* or the *ardhaparyaṅka*.

## SALIHUNDAM

It lies on the right bank of the river Vamsadhara in Śrīkakulam district and 12 kms. away from Kalingapatnam an ancient port town. There are regular buses from Śrīkakulam town. The Buddhist settlement is variously known as '*Sālipēṭaka* or *Sālipeḍaka*'[125], '*Mahā Uga Pavathe*'[126](*Mahōdake Parvata*) and *Koṭṭahārama*[127] noticed on inscribed pot sherds, found at the site. An epigraph dated 1260 A.D. engraved on the temple wall of Śrīkakulam refers to this place as 'Sālivenḍam' and it was gifted to Lord Śrī Kurmanadha at Śrīkurmam by one of the subordinates of Eastern Ganga dynasty[128].

The Buddhist settlement perched on the hill top looks very imposing, overlooking the vast expanse of the river Vamsadhara. Excavations brought to light apsidal and circular *chaityagṛihas*, pillared *maṇḍapas*, *vihāras*, images of Buddha, votive stone *stūpas* and platforms, spoked *stūpas*, terracotta receptacles, a good number of inscribed Brāhmi potsherds and sculptures of Tārā, Mañjuśrī, Mārīcī etc., belonging to the Vajrayāna cult[129]. It is interesting to note that a small lithic record datable to 2nd century A.D. reads as '*dhama rāño Aśōka Siriṇo*'. This label inscription[130] seems to suggest that though the *stūpa* was originally built by the emperor Aśōka, the fact was recorded only by the ruling kings in 2nd century A.D. while renovating the *stūpa*. The Korni plates of Anantavarma Choda Ganga (12th century A.D.) mention this holy place as *Muṇḍu maṟṟu* which means the place is famous for '*muṇḍiya* monks' (clean shaven heads)[131]. It appears that this place flourished as a prominent Buddhist centre in central Kalinga region upto the medieval times i.e. 12th century A.D.

As many as twelve sculptures datable to 9th-10th centuries A.D. were discovered at the site. A few have Sanskrit inscriptions in Nagari characters inscribed on the halos and pedestals of the sculptures. In the village were found traces of stone foundations of a temple which probably housed the sculpture of Mārīcī.

**Buddha as Amitābha** (in stucco): At the foot of the hillock in the village Salihundam where tāṅtric sculptures were found A. Rea exposed another apsidal *chaitya* (24' × 12.5' high) and a broken image of seated Buddha (4' high) in *vajrāsana* on a brick platform ( 1' high × 9' length × 5'.10'' width) near the apse[132]. The image is broken across the chest. The upper portion and hands are missing (Pl. 26).

It is a very fascinating discovery in the history of Andhra Buddhism. The image was made of large size bricks and small pieces of stone in mud mortar and the final shape of the image was obtained in lime plaster. A masonry wall was provided at the back to support the huge image. Basing on the available measurements, the image appears to have stood nearly to a height of 12 ft. In the absence of other iconographical details, the fragmentary evidences available at the site suggest that the image Boddhisattva must have been placed on a lotus throne with *makara tōraṇa* or *prabhavali* and it can be identified with one of the forms of *Pancha dhyāni* Buddhas seated either in *bhūsparśa mudrā* or *dhyāna mudrā*. The identity of it is further supported by the discovery of other Mahāyāna sculptures discovered at the site.

**Mārīcī** : This life size figure (6'9" × 4'4" × 1'2") of Mārīcī, carved in red granite is in a *ālīḍha* pose standing in a chariot drawn by seven horses. The bending of right leg and outstretched left leg obviously suggest a classic example of tāṅtric form. She is three faced and six armed. The image is slightly defaced. Except for a bowl in her lower left hand and a sword in her raised right hand, the weapons in the remaining hands of the image are beyond identification due to mutilation. However, a full blown lotus flower, an arrow and a *vajra* like object are faintly seen. The upper portion of the body is decorated with jewels and ornaments. The loose under garment below the hips, hardly covered the thighs and the ends of this diagonal one, look like a folded ribbon. The lower part of the body is well clad with a thin cloth or skirt, meticulously carved and secured in position by a beautiful girdle around the loins (Pl. 27 & 27a).

She has a well decorated head-gear with ornamental halo at the back of the head. An illegible Sanskrit inscription in thirteen lines is inscribed right from the head to the end portion of the lower garment. The inscription mentions the name of a monk 'Bhadrapāla' who built the house (of Buddha) for the merit of (his) teachers both spiritual and temporal as well as (his) parents. At the end, the inscription contains the usual imprecatory clause invoking blessings.

A conventional representation of Sun and a bunch of Aśōka flowers on the right and left top corners are depicted prominently on the *prabhāmaṇḍala* of the image. At the bottom of each foot are two little figures, the symbolic representations of Vajrasattva(?). A female charioteer is prominently depicted in *lalitāsana* holding a branch of Aśōka tree in her raised left arm. The left hand is kept in akimbo. The depiction of human head shows the symbolic representation of Rāhu (?). On the lateral sides of the pedestal are, the chariot wheels depicted conventionally one on each side.[133]

According to one *Sādhana* "She is fair with three faces, three eyes and eight hands. Her right face is red and the left one is hideous boar face of blue colour. She holds thunderbolt, an elephant goad, an arrow and needle in her right hands while there are Aśōka leaf, bow, noose and *tarjani mudrā* (a menacing pose with the index finger upwards) in her left hands. She lives inside a *chaitya*. The *Dhyāni* Buddha Vairōcana sits on her tiara. Her chariot is drawn by seven pigs, the charioteer being Rāhu. She is accompanied on the east by Vattali, on the south by Vadali, on the west by Varāli and on the north by Varāhamukhi."

Among the deities emanating from Vairocana, Mārīcī appears to be the important deity that gained popularity in the Buddhist pantheon. Being the counterpart of Vairocana, she resides in the womb of a *chaitya,* since Vairocana is the Lord of temples and *stūpas*. She is the Buddhist counterpart of the Brāhmanical God Sūrya.

Longhurst identified the image as goddess of dawn, a personification of the rising Sun, while her three faces signify the three phases of the Sun at dawn, noon and dusk. The Lamas of Tibet invoke her early in the morning which suggests her connection with the Hindu God Sūrya. In China, she is known as 'queen of heavens and mother of the Dipper'.[134] At Salihundam, her chariot is drawn by seven horses instead of seven pigs. A similar example was reported from Bihar[135]. She is considered as the *Śakti* of Amitābha, the *Dhyāni* Buddha of boundless light. Interestingly, there is an image of Sūrya in the Chidambaram temple (in Tamilnadu) where the Sun God is depicted with three faces[136]. In the early images of Brāhmanical Sun-god, from Bodhagaya, Gāndhāra, Mathura and Lala Bhagat pillar show, his chariot was drawn by four horses instead of seven horses.[137]

The goddess possesses six distinct forms and sixteen *sādhanās* as described in *Sādhanamāla*. She is another manifestation of the Goddess Tārā. She is generally represented with one, three, five or six faces and eight, ten or twelve arms. Needle and string are her important symbols. Her chariot is drawn by seven boars. The iconographical features prescribed by the Buddhist texts do not appear in the present deity under-study, especially in the depiction of the *vāhana*. According to the text, her chariot is drawn by seven boars whereas the chariot of the present deity is drawn by seven horses like the Brāhmanical Sun God. She is the principal deity in the Mārīcī maṇḍala of the *Niṣpannayōgāvaḷi*[138].

A similar image having three faces and six arms was reported from Bihar. One of the faces of the Goddess is that of Sow. Representation of seven horses on the pedestal obviously suggests her solar character, the horses a veritable cognizance of the Sun-god. It appears that the representation of Mārīcī with seven horses for her chariot is the earliest iconographical form and later on horses were substituted with pigs. According to another *Sādhana*, there is a white Mārīcī with five faces, ten arms and four legs treading on Brahma, Viṣṇu and Śiva whereas there is a red Mārīcī with six hands and twelve arms. She is seated on a sow and most terrifying[139]. In Japan Mārīcī is shown seated on a lotus throne supported by seven pigs. She has three heads as usual. Behind her head is a eight spoked Buddhist wheel. Some times she holds a *Chaitya*[140].

Other forms of Mārīcī are Aśōka Kānṭā, Ārya Mārīcī, Vajradhārēśvari etc. Images of Mārīcī are well preserved in Dacca and Indian Museums. Only one image from Saranath was reported.

**Mārīcī** : It is a well preserved beautiful image (3'6"×1'5"×1'0") seated on a lotus throne with right foot hanging below and resting on a lotus pedestal. Possessing a single face and six arms, she holds a bell, drum, rosary, *vajra*, sword and a bowl. Sun and two female worshippers are depicted on the pedestal. The goddess wears jewellery and ornaments. An attendant, probably a flying Gandharva is depicted on the left top corner of the sculpture (Pl. 28).

It appears that in the initial stage, number of pigs was not prescribed for drawing chariot of the Goddess. An illustration in the *Aṣṭasāhasrika Prajñā Pāramitā* manuscript shows a two handed form of Mārīcī with an inscription, reading *dvibhuja Mārīcī Chaityah*[141]. No *vāhana* was prescribed in it. In the same manuscript, the Uddiyāna form of Mārīcī was depicted with ten arms and three faces, sow face being one of the three. No *vāhana* was also given in it[142]. Getty illustrated one image of Mārīcī seated on a single pig[143], whereas, Clark showed two images seated on two pigs[144]. An illustration in *Dhāraṇi Saṁgraha* manuscript shows Mārīcī a seated on a chariot drawn by four pigs[145]. whereas Gordon and Getty showed the images seated on chariot drawn by five pigs[146]. In the *Sādhanamāla,* it is mentioned that her chariot was drawn by seven pigs.[147]

Thus the representation of various forms of Mārīcī does not occur in the initial stages and later on appear seated on either one, two, four, five or seven pigs to her chariot which does not correspond to any textual descriptions. Usually, the north-Indian images show chariots drawn by seven pigs whereas south-Indian images show early iconographical features with or without *vāhanas* and some times with the horses instead of pigs to her chariot.

**Vāgīśvara** : Three sculptures of Vāgīśvara carved in red granite, in different sizes were reported from the site. They are more or less identical, except for the lions shown in different positions on the pedestals.

This image of Vāgīśvara (2'2"×1'6"×10") is represented with two hands and seated in *ardhaparyaṅkāsana* on the lotus throne. At either end of the pedestal are seen two lions in recumbent posture and in the middle is a lady worshipper, holding a lamp in both the hands, in kneeling position. On the back of the throne is a *stūpa* and above it are garland bearers. He wears plenty of jewellery in addition to princely ornaments (Pl.29). The Buddhist creed formula in Sanskrit is inscribed on the halo of the image. Both the arms are broken and missing. However, the stem of the *utpala* in his left broken arm and the intact right arm disposed in graceful attitude clearly suggests that it belongs to the family of Bōdhisattva Mañjuśrī.

Longhurst[148] identified this sculpture as that of Bōdhisattva Avalōkitēśvara. Krishna Murthy[149] identified it as Mañjuśrī. But a close examination of the image, such as the representation of the lion as a *vāhana* on the pedestal, the seated posture of the deity and other iconographical details reveals, that it is none other than Vāgīśvara. The *dhyāna* in the *Sādhanamāla* describes him as follows :[150]

*Pañcavīrakaśekharaṁ kumāraṁ sarvabharanabhūṣitaṁ kuṅkumārunaṁ vāmenotpalaṁ dakṣiṇena lilayā sthitam siṁhāsanasthāṁ ātmānam kumārarūpena cintayet ....... Ōṁ Vāgīśvara Mūḥ.*

'Vāgīśvara whose head is beautiful by the images of the five *dhyāni* Buddhas is in the complexion of *kuṅkuma* and decorated with princely ornaments. He holds the blue lotus in the left hand, while his right hand is depicted artistically, in a graceful manner. Riding the lion, exhibits a princely status.'

Vāgīśvara as a tutelary deity is worshipped in Tibet and Nepal[151]. An image of Vāgīśvara in the Indian Museum holds a bell in the right hand[152]. The other two figures here, are more or less similar to the above one except for the disposition of lions on the pedestal.

**Khasarpaṇa** : He is one of the emanations of *dhyāni* Buddha Amitābha. This sculpture made on lime stone is much weathered and mutilated. He is seated in *ardhaparyaṅkāsana,* on a double lotus. His right hand is mutilated, but the posture suggests that he is in *abhayamudrā*. His left hand as usual holds the stem of the lotus (Pl. 30). Since the head is defaced, the effigy of Amitābha is not visible. He is decked with all sorts of ornaments[153]. Krishna Murthy, examined the sculpture and identified the companions of Khasarpaṇa around his head[154].The *dhyāna* described in *Sādhanamāla*[155] is as follows :

*Atmānām Bhagavantaṁ dhyāyāt himakarakoṭikiraṇāvadātaṁ dehaṁ, ūrdhvajaṭāmukuṭaṁ Amitābhaśekharaṁ viśvanalinaniṣaṇṇaṁ śaśimaṇḍale, ardhaparyaṅkaniṣaṇṇaṁ sakalālankāradharavigrahaṁ smeramukhaṁ dvīraṣṭavarṣadeśiyaṁ dakṣ iṇe varadakaraṁ vāmakareṇa sanālakamaladharaṁ, karavigalatpīyūsadhārābhyavahārarasikaṁ tadadhaḥ samāro-pitordhvamukhaṁ mahākukṣiṁ atikṛśaṁ atiśitivarnaṁ Sūcīmukhaṁ tarpayantaṁ śrīmat-Potalakācalodaranivāsinaṁ karunāsnigdhavilokanaṁ śrngārarasaparyupāsitaṁ atiśāntaṁ nānālakṣanālaṅkṛtaṁ. Tasya puratas-Tārā dakṣinapārśve Sudhanakūmāraḥ.*

*Tatra tārā śyāmā, vāmakaravidhrtaṁ sanālaṁ utpalaṁ dakṣiṇa karena vikāśayanti nānālaṅkāravati abhinavayauvanodbhinnakucabhārā, Sudhanakumāraśca kṛtāñjaliputaḥ kanakāvabhāsidyutiḥ, kumārarūpadhāri vāmakakṣavinyastapustakaḥ sakalālankāravan. Paścime Bhṛkuṭī Hayagrīva uttare.Tatra Bhṛkuṭī caturbhujā hemaprabhā jatākalāpini, vāme tridaṇḍika- maṇḍaludhārihastā dakṣiṇe vandanābhinayāksasūtradharakarā trinetrā Hayagrīvo raktavarṇaḥ kharvalambodaraḥ urddhvajvalatpingalakeśah bhujagayajñōpavitī kapilataraśmasruśreni-paricitamukhamaṇḍalaḥ raktavartulatrinetrah bhṛkuṭīkutilabhrūkaḥ vyāghra-carmāmbaraḥ daṇḍāyudhaḥ dakṣiṇakareṇa vandanābhinayī.*

*Ete sarva eva svanāpyakānanapreritadṛṣṭayo yathāsobhaṁ avasthitā-ścintanīyāḥ. Iti Khasarpaṇasādhanaṁ.*

'Khasarpana wears a *Jaṭāmakuṭa* (crown of matted hair), holds the image of Amitābha on his head, and sits on the moon shown over a double lotus in the *ardhaparyaṅka* attitude. He is decked with all sorts of ornaments, has a smiling face, exhibits *varada* pose in the right hand, and holds the lotus with its stem in the left. He is an expert in distributing the stream of nectar that flows from his hand, and *Sūcīmukha* who stands below with an uplifted face, a protruding belly and very pale appearance. He resides in the womb of the mount Potalaka, looks beautiful with compassion, is full of *Sṛiṅgāra* (amour). Extremely peaceful, he is endowed with various auspicious marks.

Before him is Tārā and to the right is Sudhanakamāra. To the west of the god is Bhṛkuṭi and to the north Hayagriva. All these deities should be meditated upon as prescribed in a befitting and artistic manner, with their eyes directed towards the face of the principal deity.'

He is also known as Khasarpaṇa Lōkanātha. The only iconographical difference between Khasarpaṇa and Lōkanātha lies in the depiction of companions. The best example of the image was reported from Pargana of Vikrampur in East Bengal[156]. Images of Khasarpaṇa were also reported both from Tibet and China[157].

**Tārā (Ārya Tārā)** : The image of Tārā (2'10"×1'.9"×10") beautifully carved in granite, is represented with two hands. Seated in *lalitāsana* on a lotus throne, she holds a lotus in her left hand while the right hand is in *varada mudrā*. She is seated cross legged with the right foot hanging down and resting on a lotus pedestal. She is richly ornamented with jewellery (Pl. 31). Her hair is done upwards and tied into the shape of an elevated bun. She is not accompanied by any God or Goddess and hence is identified as Ārya Tārā, one of the forms of Green Tārā. The pedestal is depicted with two female worshippers and lotus flower motifs[158]. An inscription in Nagari characters on the pedestal records the usual Buddhist recitation beginning with '*ye dharma'.* Such Buddhist creed formulae inscribed on stone sculptures and also in bronze icons were reported from Amaravati[159] and Guntupalli[160] in Andhra Pradesh, Kandhar in Nanded district of Mahārastra[161] and also from Khailkair in Dacca district of East Bengal[162].

The *maṁtra* prescribed to worship 'Tārā is '*ōṁ Tārā Tuttāre Ture Svāhā*. As there are several Tārās mentioned in the Buddhist literature, it is difficult to identify the particular form of Tārā from which she emanated. Some of the sculptures and paintings show an effigy of Amōghasiddhi. Among the emanations of *Dhyāni* Buddha, Amōghasiddhi is the only male, while others are feminine. She is the *Śakti* of Avalōkitēśvara *(Padmapāṇi Priyē)*. Basing on colour, the images of Tārā are classified into five categories *viz.* green Tārā, white Tārā, yellow Tārā, blue Tārā and red Tārā and ascribed to their respective *kulas* or families presided over by the five *Dhyāni* Buddhas. She is the most popular deity among the northern Buddhists and her name is a favourite personal name for women.

There are several legends about the origin of Tārā. The most accepted legend is that while Tārā was born from a tear which fell from the right eye while the green Tārā from a tear of the left eye of Avalōkitēśvara[163]. In the *Sragdharāstōtra*[164], composed by *Sarvajñamitra* (8th c. A.D) mentions the *Aṣṭamahābhaya* aspect of Tārā, in which she is invoked for deliverance from the eight perils like shipwreck, conflagration, enraged elephant, brigand, pouncing lion, serpent, prison and demon.

The *Dhāraṇi Saṁgraha*[165] mentions her as the saviour of ten worlds when the people were in distress caused by the Yakṣas and Rākṣasas. In a *dhyāna* found in *Pañcakara* section of *Advayavajra Saṁgraha*, she is mentioned as Tāriṇi. The green Tārā is the spiritual consort of Amōghasiddhi. The *dhyāna* prescribed for her worship is as follows[166]:

*Aisānyaṁ candramaṅdalopari kanakasyāma-Tāṁ kāraparinatā Tārini syāmavarnā syamnīloptala cihna vāyudhātusvarūpa karmakulā irsyāraktā.*

'In the Īśāna (north-east) corner of the orb of the moon, there is Tārini originating from the green syllable Tāṁ of golden green colour. Her symbol is a green night lotus. She is the embodiment of air. She belongs to the *karma* family and is full of jealousy'.

Several inscriptions from Karnataka record the worship of Tārā. A record of 1065 A.D., mentions the establishment of the Jayanti Pra Bauddha *Vihāra* at Balligave (Belgam) and the grant of some donations for the maintenance of this *Vihāra* and also the worship of Tārā[167]. Another inscription from Dambal (Dharwar district) dated 1095 A.D. during the reign of the Western Chalukyan king Vikramāditya[168], records grants to the temple of Tārā by some merchants. Tārā figures were also reported from Nagapattanam in Tamilnadu[169].

**Sita Tārā** (white Tārā) : Though the sculpture is found abraded, it is the best specimen carved beautifully in granite. The image (5'×2'6"×1'2") is four armed sitting cross legged in the *padmāsana* on a double lotus throne. There is a large plain halo behind her head. She holds a flower in her upper left hand and a round object *cintāmaṇi* in the lower left hand (Pl. 32). The right upper hand is broken while the lower shows *varada mudrā*.[170] Basing on iconographical features i.e. the presence of *cintāmaṇi* in one of her hands, the sculpture is identified as Sita-Tārā, inspite of the absence of her companions as described in the Buddhist texts. She has elongated ear-lobes and a conical head-gear. She is richly ornamented with jewellery, a prominent *yajñōpavīta* and an under-garment. She is generally represented with the third eye suggesting fore-knowledge. Due to mutilation of the sculpture this feature is lost.

Sita Tārā is one of the four deities that emanated from combination of the five *Dhyāni* Buddhas, the other three being Vajratārā, Prajñā Pāramita and Kurukuḷḷa. The *Sādhanamāla* describes her form as follows :[171]

*Tārābhagavatāṁ śuklaṁ trinetrāṁ caturbhujāṁ Pañca-Tathāgatamukutīṁ nānālankārāṁ, bhujadvayena utpalamudrāṁ dadhānāṁ, dakṣiṇabhujena cintāmaṇiratnasaṁyuktavaradāṁ, sarvasattvānāṁ āśāṁ paripūryantīṁ, vāmenotpalamañjarīṁ vibhrāṇaṁ dhyāyāt. Tasyā dakṣinṇpārśve Mārīcīṁ pitāṁ candrāsanāṁ nilāmbarāṁ dvibhujāṁ; vāmena raktāśokapallavadharāṁ, dakṣiṇena sitacāmara dharāṁ raktakañcukābharanāṁ. Vāmapārśve Mahāmāyūriṁ priyaṅguśyāmāṁ dvibhujāṁ; vāmena mayūra picchadharāṁ, dakṣiṇena cāmaradharāṁ, evaṁ vicīntya .*

'Sita Tārā is white complexioned, having three eyes and four arms. She bears the images of the five *Dhyāni* Buddhas on her crown decked with many ornaments. It exhibits *utpala mudrā* with the first pair of hands and displays *varada mudrā* along with the *cintāmaṇi* jewel, shown in the second right, carries the *utpala* bud in the second left, and fulfils the prayers of all beings. To her right is Mārīcī and on her left is Mahāmayūri.'

Though the present image understudy is devoid of companions, the iconographical features agree with the description given in *Sādhanamāla*. The tāṅtric form of Sita-Tārā is Janguli-Tārā, the dispeller of poison who is invoked to cure serpent stings.[172] She is the consort of Avalōkitēśvara. She symbolizes purity and represents transcendent wisdom. Images of this type were reported from Tibet and China and also from Dacca Museum.

**Maitrēya** : Though, it is a broken sculpture with the lower portion missing, the iconographical features in the upper portion is well depicted. He holds the *nāgakēśara* flower in his left hand and a *chāmara* in his right hand. He wears *makarakuṇḍalas, yajñōpavīta* and a *kanṭhābharaṇa*. He is in smiling attitude with an elaborate and decorated head gear (Pl. 33). A well preserved image of Maitrēya was also reported from Amaravati[173].

**Padmapāṇi** : It is a mutilated one. The head portion is broken and missing. He stands in *samabhanga* attitude on a lotus. He holds a long stem of the lotus in his left hand while the right is in *bhūmisparśa mudrā*. He is decorated with the usual ornaments. The part below the waist is well clad with a thin loin cloth, the folds of which touch the anklets (Pl. 34).

He is the emanation of *Dhyāni* Buddha Akṣobhya belonging to the lotus family. His spiritual consort is Pandara. He is red in colour and a full blown lotus is his symbol. Padmapāṇi is well represented in all South Asian countries. Sculptures of this deity are reported from Amaravati,[174] Gummadidurru[175] etc.

**Buddha** : Out of seven sculptures of Buddha reported from the site, three depict Buddha in *bhūsparśa mudrā* (Akṣobhya) seated in *vajraparyaṅkāsana* and flanked by Maitrēya (Pl. 35 & 36). The remaining sculptures are Buddha in *Dhyāna* mudrā (Amitābha).

**(a) Buddha *in Bhūsparśa mudrā* :** It is a broken image (5'6" × 2'0" × 1'6") carved in granite stone. The halo is inscribed with Buddhist creed formula.[176] On the pedestal are two recumbent lions, one at each end with a Bōdhisattva in the middle. Over and above the throne is a chowri-bearer[176].

**(b) Buddha in *Dhyāna mudrā* :** He is seated in *padmasana* (4'6" × 2'0" × 1'2") in *dhyāna mudrā* attitude. Both the hands are kept clapsed. At the base of the throne are three lions. On either side of the figure on the top are Maitrēyas[177]. The *cūṛnakuṅtala* and *uṣṇīṣas* are prominently depicted.

**Mañjuśrī :** The sculpture of Mañjuśrī (2'2" × 1'×6" × 10") seated on lotus throne in *ardhaparyaṅkāsana* is meticulously carved in red sand stone (Pl. 37). It is slightly mutilated. The pedestal is depicted with recumbent lions and an attendant. The inscribed halo is partly broken. He is seated in the attitude usually called 'royal ease' (*Mahārājalila* Mañjuśrī) with the right knee lifted, over which hangs the right arm, the left leg is bent while the left hand holds the stem of *utpala*[178].

According to the accepted legend, he was born of a golden ray from the forehead of Gautama Buddha, which pierced a Jambu-tree. A lotus sprang from the tree and from the interior of the flower was born the prince of sages, Ārya Mañjuśrī. He is yellow in colour, with one face and two arms. The right hand holds a sword while the left hand carries a book or a stem of *utpala*. He is endowed with superior and inferior marks of beauty[179].

Mañjuśrī belongs to the group of eight *Dhyāni* Bōdhisattvas and is represented with all the Bōdhisattva ornaments[180]. An effigy of Akṣobhya is seen in his crown. His *uṣṇīṣa* is ornamented at the top by a flaming pearl. Mañjuśrī bears several names such as Mañjuvajra, Mañjughoṣa and Dharmadhātu Vāgīśvara. He, the soft beautied one Mañjughoṣa, the mellow-voiced one is commonly known as the Buddhist God of learning and culture. A book, a sword and a blue lotus are his special symbols. He has two distinct types as per the *Sādhana*, one with the sword and book and the other with the *utpala* or blue lotus.

According to the Chinese Buddhist sources, the Bōdhisattva Mañjuśrī was informed by Gautama Buddha that it was the duty to turn the wheel of Law for the salvation[181]. His name occurs for the first time in the *Āryamañjuśrī Mūlakalpa*, which is earlier than *Gūhya samāja* (300 A.D)[182]. Forty one *sādhanās* in the *Sādhanamāla* are devoted to the worship of Mañjuśrī. His name is described in

*Lōkanāth Sādhana* of the *Sādhanamāla*[183] as *Mañjughōṣāli kanakabhaḥ Khaḍga Pustaka dhārakaḥ* 'Mañjughōṣa is of golden colour and he holds in his two hands the sword and the book.'

In *Niṣpannayōgāvaḷi*[184], he is described as *Pitanilaśuklasavyetaravaktraḥ ṣaḍbhujo dakṣiṇaiḥ khaḍgavaradabānān vāmaih prajñapāramitā pustaka nilābjadhanuṁṣi bibhrāṇaḥ.*

'Mañjuśrī has three faces in yellow, blue and white colours. He is six armed. In the three right arms he holds the sword, *varada mudrā* and the arrow and in the three left carries the *Prajñāpāramita* book, the blue lotus and the bow.'

He is a very popular deity in China[185]. Several images of Mañjuśrī are found in Dacca Museum[186]. A rare specimen in Baroda Museum shows Mañjuśrī in the company of two principal Hindu Gods, Gaṇapati and Viṣṇu[187].

## GUNTUPALLI

It is a famous Buddhist site known for its unique caves and exuberant rock-cut architecture in Eastern Deccan. It is located 10 kms. west of Kamavarapukota and 45 kms. to the north of Eluru Railway Station in the West Godavari District. Locally, it is known as Gundupalle. The site was reported first by Robert Sewell[188] in 1882, and later on excavated partly by Alexander Rea[189], who called it as 'Nagulapalle'. Subsequently, A.H. Longhurst[190] in 1916 brought to light the votive *stūpas* circular *chaityagṛihas,* Brāhmi label inscriptions etc. I.K. Sarma identifies this monastic complex with '*Mahānāgaparvata*' mentioned in one of the Brahmi label inscriptions discovered at the site[191].

The rock-cut caves here consist of simple rectangular halls, with cells in a row. The entrances were decorated with arched facades. The monastic establishment comprises of a circular *chaitya* with a *stūpa*, brick *stūpas*, a circular brick *chaitya*, a four pillared congregation hall, an apsidal Buddha *chaitya*, votive *stūpas* etc. Other cultural materials of the site include *maṇḍapa* pillars incised with inscriptions belonging to the time of Mahā-mēghavāhana Sirisada in Brahmi characters, early historic pottery, bronze icons, relic caskets, Buddha images etc. all chronologically ranging in date between 3rd-2nd centuries B.C. and 9th-10th centuries A.D. The available cultural materials here, suggest that this complex continued upto 10th-11th centuries A.D. as a renowned Buddhist centre in the Vengi region, affiliated first to Mahāyāna sect and afterwards to Vajrayāna.

In the south-western slope of the middle terrace of the hillock is a small rectangular cave with a sloping roof. The cave faces east and it has a rectangular opening. The interior side walls are marked by plain arched empty niches. The cave is filled with debris. The verandah is paved with Cuddapah slabs which were inscribed with Brāhmi label inscriptions datable to 1st century A.D. The front cave and top are covered by fallen brick walls of a monastic unit of a later period. In the course of removal of debris and fallen bricks, were noticed a replica of *stūpa* in terracotta, relic caskets and a fine bronze icon of Bōdhisattva Padmapāṇi[192].

**Padmapāṇi :** This two handed icon (15.5 × 8 × 8 cms.) is *seated* in *rājalīlāsana* on *padmapīṭha*. A decorated *prabhāmaṇḍala* crowned by a *chhatravali* clearly indicates that the icon was under worship. His left hand holds the stem of a lotus and his right hand is in *varada mudrā*. A devotee in meditative posture is shown on the left side of the pedestal (Pl. 38). On the lotus pedestal is a Buddhist creed formula reading "*Ye-dharma hētu prabhavaḥ hētun tēśām tathāgatō hyavādat Tēṣ anchāye nirōdha ēyam vadi Mahā sramaṇaḥ*" in Nagari characters datable to 9th-10th centuries A.D. It means that the 'Tathāgata has revealed the cause of those phenomena which spring from a cause and also (the means of) their cessation. So says the monk.' The *ślōka* gives the essence of the teachings of the Buddha. Another Buddhist creed formula is found engraved on the stone tablet reading "*Dukha Dukhi Samutpadaṁ Dukhasya Vavetikkram Ariyañcha ajaṁgikaṁ ma tīṁ Dukhōpaśama Samikam*". Such Buddhist creed formulae inscribed on the sculptures are reported from Salihundam[193] and Amaravati[194] in Andhra Pradesh, Khandhar in Maharastra[195] and also Khailkair in East Bengal[196]. Seated images are found commonly in China[197].

Padmapāṇi is the spiritual emanation of the *Dhyāni* Buddha Amitābha belonging to the lotus family. According to Buddhist tradition, after the death of Gautama Buddha, Padmapāṇi appears to have taken the process of propagation of Buddhism until the creation of fifth world by Viśvapāṇi. He is also the favourite deity of the Nāgas[198]. Probably, this was the reason to get more sculptures and icons of Padmapāṇi from south-east coastal areas of Andhra Pradesh which happened to be the ancient land of Nāgas. Images were reported from Salihundam, Amaravati, Goli, Nandayapalem, Gummadidurru, Buddham, Nelakondapalli, Ramatirtham etc. in A.P.

Here, the presence of the relic caskets along with the bronze icon is worth noting. Probably, the relics were consecrated underneath the image of Padmapāṇi for worship. Such instances are also reported from Nagarjunakonda[199] where relics were consecrated in the *padmapīṭha* of a standing Buddha idol. The above evidences clearly suggest that the monastic complex existed as a seat of Vajrayāna Buddhism atleast from 6th-7th centuries A.D. onwards.

## GUMMADIDURRU

It is a small village, about 10 kms. from Madhira, on Vijayawada-Hyderabad railway line. It lies about 1 km. north of Ramareddipalle and 9 kms. east of the famous Buddhist site-Jaggayyapeta in Nandigama taluk of Krishna district. Excavations (1926) brought to light an extensive Buddhist settlement, comprising a *Mahāstūpa*, votive *stūpas*, apsidal *chaityagṛihas* and other secular and religious sculptures. The plan and construction of the *Mahāstūpa* is quite interesting. It is 55 ft. in dia and rises to a height of 4 ft. with four *āyaka* projections (13 x 4 x 2 ft.). On plan, it appears to be wheel shaped. Its central part is in the form of *swastika* with a square hub in the centre. The cultural milieu includes sculptured panels, beads, two lead coins of Sātavāhana period, a relic casket and early historic pottery. The discovery of an inscription datable to 2nd century A.D. engraved on a votive *stūpa* and one hundred and twenty seven clay tablets, incised with Buddhist creed formulae in Nagari characters of late medieval period[200], clearly suggest a prolonged activity at the site. Some of the seals bear a longer legend stamped with a row of five *stūpas* or pagodas on the top. Similar Buddhist creed formulae were reported from Sankaram and Salihundam. A sculpture of Padmapāṇi was reported from the site.

**Padmapāṇi :** He is also known as Bōdhisattva Avalōkitēśvara, standing on a lotus pedestal represented with two hands. The left hand holds the stem of *Nāgakēśari* or lotus bud and the right hand is in *bhūmisparśa or varada mudrā*. On the top of *chhatravali* or parasol is an effigy of the *Dhyāni* Buddha Amitābha parental *Dhyāni* Buddha (Pl.39). On his left side is a *vajra* or thunderbolt. On the inscribed lotus pedestal are seated deers and a monk kneeling in *añjali* posture. The Sanskrit inscription on the pedestal dated to 8th-9th c. A.D. reads as follows[201]:

*Svati Ācārya Mougalyā yanasya priya-śiṣyasya Ācārya.*
*(Dha)ramma-devasya Śisyena Śramaneka Rāhulena Bhagavath.*
*Pratimā Pratista pitā sarva satvā manuttarāyi.*
*Avāpateye yadattra punyam sarvaṁ caitya-saṁghasya.*

It records 'the consecration of the image of the Lord by a *Śramaṇa* named Rāhula, a disciple of Ācārya Dharmmadēva, a favourite disciple of Ācārya Mauggalayana.

The discovery of clay tablets bearing Buddhist creed formulae in association with Vajrayāna sculptures appears to be a noteworthy feature in South-Indian Buddhist sites. The practice of incising clay tablets with formulae of Buddhist creed was prevalent in North Indian *stūpas*. At Paharpur and Mainmati, thousands of tiny unburnt clay *stūpas*, encasing clay tablets have been reported from the *stūpas*. Several *stūpas* at Ratnagiri yielded terracotta plaques and stone slabs bearing *dharaṇis*[202]. Similarly at Gilgil in Kāshmir manuscripts, votive clay *stūpas*, tiny tablets inscribed with the Buddhist creed and other stone plaques weer recovered from a *stūpa*[203].

The concept behind the insertion of *dharaṇis* inside the *stūpas* is explained in an inscription found in Orissa, according to which, the person who constructs a *chaitya* with a deposit of *dharaṇi* inside, is equal to the one who erected one lakh *Tathāgata Chaityas*[204].

## KUNTHURU

An idol of Lord Buddha as Amitābha (1.70 × 0.90 mts.) carved out of granite stone, seated on a lotus pedestal was reported from Kunthuru, a hamlet of Koradi, located 15 kms. north-east of Sullurupet in Nellore district. The presence of brick bats in and around the find spot obviously suggests that the idol was once housed in a brick built structure[205].

**Buddha as Amitābha :** He is shown seated in *ardhapadmāsana* with hands placed in *dhyāna mudrā* (meditative pose) on a pedestal which is depicted with lotus and lion motifs (Pl. 40). The garment flowing from left shoulder to cover chest portion appears like a band of cloth rather than the multiple folds as normally seen in the sculptures of Amaravati and Nagarjunakonda. There is a *prabhāvaḷi* behind the sculpture. *Makaras* on either side of the head are shown emanating stylised creepers through their wide open mouths. The head with curly hair and prominent protruberance on the cranium or *uṣṇīṣa* issues a tongue of flames a rare form so far not reported particularly from North and mid coastal areas of Āndhradēśa. On iconographical features, it is dated to 12th-13th centuries A.D. Such images were reported from Nagapattanam, Tiruvatti, Elaiyur in Tamilnadu[206] and Kollapattu (Damarai) in Nellore district of A.P.[207] This form of Amitābha is stated in the *Pañcakara* section of the *Advaya Vajra Saṁgraha* as follows[208] :

*Paścimadaḷē Ravimaṇḍalōpari Rakta-Hṛiḥ karasaṁbhūta raktavarnō Amitābhah padmachinah samādhimudrādharaḥ Saṁjñāskandhasvābhavō rāga śarīraḥ śukrātmakali Padmakuli Pratyavēksa najñānalakṣanō grīṣmaṛturupaha mālarasasarirah tatvargātmā Pradōśavān.*

'On the western petal, on the disc of the Sun is Amitābha in red colour emanating from the red syllable Hrih. His symbol is diagnostic Lotus. He is in the *samādhi mudrā*. He is the nature of the cosmic element of *saṁjña* (name), is an embodiment of attachment and belongs to the lotus family. He stands for the vital fluid and is endowed with the *pratyavēkṣana* (looking after) knowledge.'

He represents the summer season and the acid taste. He presides over the group of letters beginning with *Ta* and rules over the evening twilight. His *vāhana* is a pair of peacocks. His colour is red and symbol is lotus. He is in meditative *mudrā*. A good number of sculptures were reported from Salihundam, Amaravati and Ramatirtham. These images are abundantly found in Tibet and China[209].

## MUKHALINGAM

Mukhalingam, a famous pilgrim centre in north-coastal Āndhradēśa is situated on the left bank of the river Vamsadhara in Śrīkakulam district. According to Buddhist literature, it was the principal city in the region of ancient Kalinga, familiarily known as *Trikaḷiṅga*. Two kilometers away from Mukhaliṅgam lies an ancient place known as Nagarikaṭakam which flourished as an urban centre, like Dhānya-kaṭakam and Sālipīṭakaṁ in the early centuries of Christian era. Archaeological investigations on the banks of the river behind the Lord Madhukēśvara temple resulted in the exposure of several brick structures and early historic pottery[210] besides a Sātavāhana coin[211]. Recent renovation works near the temple complex also brought to light early historic vestiges.

In the precincts of the temples and also in the outskirts of the village were noticed three loose sculptures of Buddhist pantheon *viz*. Buddha in *bhūmisparśa mudrā* (Akṣobhya), Buddha in *dhyāna mudrā* (Amitābha) and a figure of Uṣṇīṣa Vijaya. The discovery of these Vajrayāna sculptures here, suggests that the early Buddhist establishment at Mukhaliṅgam must have survived upto the medieval times.[212]

**Buddha in bhūsparśa mudrā :** He sits on the *vajra* in *vajraparyaṅkāsana* in *bhūsparśa mudrā* on a double lotus pedestal. An oval shaped *prabhāvaḷi*, a pair of chowry bearers on either side of the head and a dwarfish Yakṣa flanked by lions on the pedestal are some of the prominent features (Pl. 41). The sculpture is carved in lime stone. It is dated to 8th-9th centuries A.D.

**Buddha in *dhyāna mudrā* :** The sculpture is made of red sand stone. He is shown seated on a lotus pedestal in *dhyāna mudrā*. A pair of *makaras* on either side of the figure at the shoulder level, flying figures holding fly whisks and a *prabhāmaṇḍala* are prominently depicted (Pl. 42).

**Uṣṇīṣa Vijaya :** The sculpture under study was once worshipped as Brahmēśvari. Presently, it is kept inside the temple located in the outskirts of the village. It is carved in red sand stone. She is seated in *vajraparyaṅkāsana* on a lotus pedestal which is depicted with attendants in *añjali*. She is three faced and eight armed. She is decked with ornaments and prominent head gears. Though, on the *prabhāvaḷi* are the representations of five *dhyāni* Buddhas, only the figure of *dhyāni* Buddha Ratnasaṁbhava is clearly seen (Pl. 43). The depiction of third eye is not clearly visible due to the heavy application of turmeric. Her four right hands display double thunderbolt (Viśvavajra ?), the arrow, the third weapon is not clear and the fourth one is in *varada* pose while her four left hands show the bow, the goad (*aṅkuśa*), the noose with the *tarjani mudrā* and a water vessel respectively.

The iconographical features of the sculpture agree with almost in all the details given in the *Sādhanamāla*, though some of the features with the image of Vajra-tārā. She is an offspring of Vairōcana who resides in the *chaitya*. There are several *dhyānas* which describe her form. One of the *dhyānas* is as follows[213] :

*Śuktaṁ trimukhaṁ trinetrāṁ navayauvanāṁ nānālaṅkara dharāṁ aṣṭabhujaṁ Bhagavatiṁ Cintayet; pītakṛṣṇadakṣiṇetaravadanāṁ; dakṣiṇacaturbhujaiḥ visvavajra-Padmastha-Buddha-bāna-Varada mudrādharāṁ, Vāmacaturbhujaiḥ cāpa-tarjanī-pāśa-abayahasta-puṛnakumbhāḥ; caitya guhāgarbhasthitāṁ, Vairōcanamukutinīṁ nispādya uṣṇīṣavijaya sādhanaṁ.*

'She is white in complexion, three faced, three eyed, youthful and is decked with many ornaments. Her right hands display the Viśvavajra, Buddha on lotus, the arrow and the *varada* pose, and her four left hands show the bow, the noose with the *tarjani*, the *abhaya* pose and well filled water vessel. She resides in the womb of the *chaitya* and bears the image of Vairōcana on the crown.'

In Japan, she is considered as the deified form of Buddha's *uṣṇīṣa*[214]. The symbols in her hands vary from one sculpture to the other. For example, instead of *abhaya* pose, she may hold a filled water vessel having a branch of Aśōka tree.[215] She is a very popular goddess in Tibet and Mangolia. She is one of the earliest feminine divinities. A fine sculpture was also reported from the collections of Indian Museum[216].

## TAKKALLAPADU

A unique sculpture of Harītī was reported from the village Takkallapadu in Jaggayyapeta mandal of Krishna district, while digging the earth for laying telephone cables. Subsequent surveys in and around the find spot resulted in discovery of early historic materials such as inscribed stone pillars with Brāhmi characters, broken sculptured panels, black and red ware, black ware, red polished ware etc., datable to the post-Sātavāhana times[217].

**Harītī :** The sculpture of (29 × 12 × 13 cms.) Harītī, made in lime stone is a rare specimen which represents the earliest form of the goddess so far reported in South-India. She is shown seated on a pedestal depicting *triratna* symbols surmounting half lotus medallions on the lateral sides and eight petalled lotus on the back side. Seated on a pedestal in *bhadrāsana*, she holds a baby in her lap with both the hands. Broad and thick nose, almond shaped eyes, thick lips and broad face are some of the characteristic features of a *Yakṣiṇi* generally seen in Ikṣvāku sculptures. She is adorned with prominent *chakra-kuṇḍalas*, simple armlets and anklets. The necklace (*kānṭhābharaṇa*) around her neck and simple coiffure are very meticulously and prominently carved (Pl. 44).

The depiction of *triratna* symbols on the pedestal obviously suggests the transformation of the Goddess from the cannibalic stage to Divine *Saṅgha* and also the position she occupaid in the Buddhist pantheon. Some scholars identified the sculpture as Maya Devi giving birth to Buddha, considering the cloth over the genitals and illegible *uṣṇīṣa* (?) which are the important *Mahāpuruṣa lakṣaṇās* ascribed to Buddha.

In Buddhist iconography, Harītī is the only goddess found holding a baby in her hands. Generally, the Mahāyānists believe that at the stage of Bōdhi only he would have acquired the thirty two superior and eighty minor marks of a Buddha. In the *Mahāvastu*, it is mentioned that all the thirty two outward signs were acquired only in his last rebirth, but Sākyamuni as a child does not show the protruberance on the skull (*uṣṇīṣa*) which is the most important feature of thirty two outward signs of a *Mahāpuruṣa*. Even as an ascetic also he was not represented with full-sized *uṣṇīṣa*. It is only after the attainment of super wisdom he was shown with fully developed *uṣṇīṣa* the receptacle, presumably of the divine mind (*manas*)[218].

Thus the sculpture from Takkallapadu in view of its iconographical features of Harītī can be dated to the Sātavāhana times. As seated image of this type, though upper portion broken was reported from Nagarjunakonda. This image from Takkallapadu happens to be the earliest representation of goddess Harītī, so far reported particularly in Andhra Pradesh and South India in general.

## RAMATIRTHAM

It is a small village about 15 kms. north-east of Vizianagaram, the headquarters of the district. On the northern side of the village lie two prominent hillocks locally known as Durgakonda and Gurubhaktakonda perched with Buddhist monasteries datable to 1st-2nd c. A.D. Excavations conducted by A. Rea unearthed brick built apsidal *chaityagrihas, vihāras*, images of Buddha in *dhyāna* and *bhūsparśa mudrā*, a lead coin, clay seals, stone votive *stūpas*, relic caskets, clay seals, iron objects etc. One of the seals contains a Brahmi legend reading '*Śrī Śiva* (*Maka*) *Vijaya Rāja Śelasaghasa*' in 2nd c. A.D. characters. It appears that the king Śiva maka Vijaya was a local Chieftain who probably ruled over this region after the eclipse of the Sātavāhana kingdom. The other cultural materials at the site suggest that the site must have survived upto 8th-9th centuries A.D.[219] Sculptures of Buddha in *dhyāna* and *bhūsparśa mudrās* are now preserved in the museum site at Salihundam in Śrīkakulam district[220].

**Buddha in *Dhyāna Mudrā* :** Made of khondalite stone he is shown seated on a pedestal in *dhyāna mudrā*. Two attendants holding fly whisks on either side at shoulder level and a disc beyond the head are prominently shown.

**Buddha in *Bhūsparśa Mudrā* :** It is a highly abraded sculpture. The features are not very clear. He is seated on pedestal in *bhūsparśa mudrā*.

## KOLLAPATTU

It is a hamlet of Damarai village located in the island of Pulicat lake in Sullurupet mandal of Nellore district. It is about 20 kms. from Sullurupet and 8 kms. from Śrīharikota—a famous space launching centre in South India. Survey in and around the village resulted in the discovery of medieval pot sherds and an image of Buddha in *dhyāna mudrā*[221]. On stylistic grounds it is datable to 12th c. A.D.

**Buddha in *dhyāna Mudrā* (Amitābha) :** It is a beautiful image (120 x 60 cms.) carved in green granite stone. He is shown seated in *vajraparyaṅkāsana* in *dhyāna mudrā* (Pl. 45). A prominent halo behind the head and *uṣṇīṣa* showing a tongue of flames are the important features representing Buddha as Amitābha. Similar images with flaming *uṣṇīṣa* are reported from Kunthuru in Nellore district in A.P[222]. Elaiyur in Tamilnadu[223] and at Awkana, Veheragala and Gadaladeniya in Śrī Laṅkā[224]. A *dhyāna* for his worship is also given in the *Advayavajra saṁgraha*[225].

## VAIKUNTHAPURAM

Nearer to the village Amaravati, a famous Buddhist centre in Guntur district, lies another early historic site in Vaikunthapuram, a small village on the right bank of the river Krishna. It is 20 kms. away from Vijayawada on Vijayawada-Amaravati road. The other known Buddhist sites nearby the village are Amaravati, Vaddamanu and Penumaka located along the same river bank. Earlier, fragments of a *hārmika*, *chhatra* carved in lime stone, rouletted ware, inscribed pot sherds, celadon ware, terracotta mould for minting punch marked coins etc., datable to 1st-2nd c. A.D. have been reported from the site.[226] Recently a sculpture of Buddha in *bhūsparśa mudrā* was recovered from the eroded bank of the river[227].

**Buddha in *bhūsparśa mudrā* (Akṣobhya) :** For the first time comes an image of Buddha carved in black basalt particularly from Buddhist sites of this region. He is shown seated in a *vajraparyaṅkāsana*, placing his left hand in *dhyāna mudrā* and the right hand in *bhūsparśa mudrā* (Pl. 46). A beautifully carved *vajra* is symbolically shown on the pedestal. The facial features though defaced, the iconographical characters tally with those images reported from Amaravati[228] and Salihundam[229]. On stylistic grounds it is datable to 9th-10th c. A.D. Buddha in *bhūsparśa mudrā* is generally known as Akṣobhya and a *dhyāna* for his worship is mentioned in the *Advayavajra saṁgraha*[230].

## NANDAYAPALEM

It is an extensive early historic habitation site located approximately about 5 kms. away from Chandavolu in Guntur district. The habitation area spreads over the present villages of Karlapalem, Etravaripalem and Buddham. While digging the soil for agricultural purpose, a good number of sculptured panels, brick structures, sculptures with Brāhmi label inscriptions and early historic pottery datable to 1st-2nd c. A.D. were recovered from the habitation. All the sculptures were shifted to the Boudha Sri Archaeological Museum, Guntur. In the collection, was found an image of Bhōdhisattva Padmapāṇi a fascinating one[231].

**Padmapāṇi :** This sculpture carved in lime stone shows Padmapāṇi standing in *samabhaṅga* attitude on a lotus pedestal decked with traditional Bōdhisattva dress and ormanents. His left hand is kept on the waist (*kaṭihastha*) while his right hand holds a full blown lotus (Pl. 47). He is in graceful attitude. He has a three tiered semi-circular head gear. There are a pair of attendants, on each side, carved very meticulously; a male dwarf attendant (*yakṣa*) holding *chhatravali* (broken and missing), a pair of attendants in *añjali mudrā* and an attendant with basket of flowers. Some scholars identified it as Siddhartha in royal costumes. A full blown lotus in his right hand, obviously suggests that it was the representation of Buddha as Bōdhisattva Padmapāṇi. Similar images were reported from Goli—a Buddhist site in Guntur district, Andhra Pradesh[232] and also Ceylon[233]. Though, a non-Tāntric form, it was favoured by the Vajrayānists of South east-Asian countries.

## BUDDHAM

Buddham, a famous early historic site known for its rich Buddhist remnants, is a road side village on Guntur-Bapatla high way. It is 60 kms. from Guntur town and 18 kms. from Bapatla in Guntur district. The present village itself is built on the ancient habitation. Periodical diggings here, brought to light brick structures, sculptured panels, Brahmi label inscriptions and early historic pottery datable to the Sātavāhana times[234]. One such diggings at this site yielded a pair of bronze icons of Padmapāṇi dated to 2nd-3rd c. A.D. on stylistical grounds.

**Padmapāṇi :** These are the earliest bronze icons (43.5 cm. height) reported from South India datable to the Sātavāhana times. He is shown standing in *samabhaṅga*, attitude holding stalk of a lotus or *nāgakēśara* flower (bud) in his left hand while his right hand is kept in *varada mudrā* (Pl. 48). He is decked with traditional Bōddhisattva dress and ornamentation[235]. His head gear is very meticulously carved with small curls of hair shaped into a conical bun without showing prominent *uṣṇīṣa*. His oval face, pointed nose, elongated ear lobes, closed lips and drapery show close similarities with the sculptures of Gandhara region. Similar bronze icons of early medieval period were reported from Amaravati[236] and Nelakondapalli[237] in Andhra Pradesh.

## NELAKONDAPALLI

It is a road side village on Khammam-Kodada highway, familiarly known as the birth place of the Saint Kancherla Gopanna (*Bhakta* Ramadas)—the architect of the famous Rama temple at Bhadrachalam in Khammam district. It is an ancient fortified city comprising numerous mounds inside. Excavations at the early historic mounds in the village locally known as *Vīratarāja dibba* and *Biragula Gutta* brought to light a number of lime stone images of standing Buddha, a row of brick built water troughs for the treatment of sculptured panels, *vihāras*, a *mahāchaitya*, rock-cut votive *stūpas*, terracotta figures besides numerous Viṣṇukuṇḍin coins (4th-5th c. A.D.). The presence of uncarved lime stone blocks, chips and flakes at *Biragulagutta* obviously suggests that it was a manufacturing centre of Buddhist sculptures and panels. Recently an icon of standing Buddha as Padmapāṇi in bronze was brought to light by the fishermen of the village from the rivulet nearby, flowing adjacent to the *Biragulagutta*. On stylistic grounds, it is dated to the post-Gupta times (6th c. A.D.).

**Avalōkiteśvara :** It is the earliest bronze icon of Buddha generally known as Padmapāṇi, made in a solid mould reported from the Viṣṇukuṇḍin habitation in

Andhra Pradesh. He is shown standing in *samabhaṅga* with two hands (Pl. 49). The right hand is shown in *varada mudrā*, while his left hand holds the stem of a *nāgakēśara* flower or lotus bud (Pl. 50a). He looks very simple wearing traditional ornamentation and Bōdhisattva dress. His inner garment and drapery clearly show the influence of Gāndhāra style of art. The *urṇa* on the forehead, long ear lobes and *uṣṇīṣa* resembling a bun on the cranium are prominently and meticulously moulded[238]. Interestingly, the *urṇa* and the eyes are inlaid with silver (Pl. 50b).

According to his *mantra* '*ōṁ maṇi padme hūṁ*', he should carry a jewel; but so far no example of this type was reported[239]. Padmapāṇi is a non-tāntric form of Avalōkitēśvara. His spiritual father is Amitābha. He is the favourite deity of the *Nāgas* (Serpent Gods)[240]. Images of Padmapāṇi are also reported from Gummadidurru, Amaravati, Salihundam and Buddham in Andhra Pradesh.

Several icons and images of Vajrayāna phase of Buddhism reported from various parts of Andhradēśa chronologically belonged to the early period as against the forms reported from Tamilnadu and Karnataka and those images reported from the northern, central and eastern India. Most of the forms may not exactly correspond to the *Sādhanas* mentioned in several Tantric Texts, because some of the images might have been conceived in their primitive iconometric forms, prior to the compilation of the Taṅtric texts. Taṅtric and non-Taṅtric forms devoid of ornamentation and coupled with literary evidences obviously, suggest obviously the early roots of Vajrayāna phase of Buddhism in Andhradēśa.

## REFERENCES


1. D.C. Sircar, *Op.cit.,* 1965, p. 36.
2. *Ibid.,* pp. 38-41.
3. B. Subrahmanyam, *Buddhist Relic Caskets in South India,* Delhi, 1998, pp. 3-4.
4. *EI,* Vol. II, p. 328.
5. T.V.G. Sastry, *Op.cit.,* 1988, pp. 4-5.
6. *ARIE,* 1953-54, No. 57, pp. 3, 21 and 25.
7. D. Jitender Das, "Influence of Andhra Buddhism in Northern Karnataka" a paper presented at the National Seminar on Buddhist Culture in Āndhradēśa, held on 17-18 May 2000, Hyderabad.
8. S. Dutt, *Buddhist Monks and Monasteries in India,* 1960, p. 120 and also see N. Dutt, *Early Monastic Buddhism,* 1941, pp. 193-95.
9. T. Ramachandra and B. Venkata Ramanayya, (Telugu trans.) *Lalitha Vistharam,* 1969, pp. 9-10.
10. *Ibid.,* p. 9.
11. N.S. Ramachandra Murthy, '*Excavations at Kōṭaliṅgāla in Karimnagar Dist., A.P.* (Unpublished report), Archaeology and Museums, Hyderabad, 1990.

12. *AAR,* A & M, Hyd. 1988-89, (cyclostyled copy).
13. *EI.,* Vol. II, p. 328.
14. T.V.G. Sastry and Others, *Vaddamanu Excavations,* Hyd., 1988, p. 4.
15. *ARIE,* 1953-54, No. 57, pp. 3, 21 and 35.
16. I.K. Sarma, 'Some More Inscriptions from Amaravati Excavations and the Chronology of the Mahāstūpa' *JESI,* Vol. I, 1974, pp. 60-74.
17. D.C. Sarcar, *Select Inscriptions,* 1965, pp. 50-52.
18. *EI,* XXXV, pp. 211-218.
19. *EI,* XX, pp. 22-23.
20. *EI,* VI, pp. 84-89.
21. B.S.L. Hanumantha Rao and etal., *Buddhist Inscriptions of Āndhradēśa,* Hyderabad, 1988, pp. 191-93.
22. M. Rama Rao, Buddhism and Buddhist Monuments in A.P. in *Buddha Jayanti Souvenir*, 1956, pp. 7-10.
23. Michael Lock Wood and Vishnu Bhatt, *Mattavilasa Prahāsana,* Madras, 1981, pp. 43-45.
24. *EI,* Vol. VI, p. 155.
25. N.Venkata Ramanayya, *Inscriptions of Andhra Pradesh,* Warangal district, 1974, pp. 45-50.
26. *JAHRS*, Vol. XXIX, part (3 & 4), p. 24.
27. *Epigraphia Zeylanica,* Vol. IV, 1943, pp. 90 ff.
28. *ARAD,* 1926-27, pp. 156-57.
29. B. Subrahmanyam, "Excavations at Gopalapatnam" in *A.A.R.* 1993-94, A.R.M., Hyderabad.
30. B. Bhattacharya (Ed), *Sādhanamāla*, G.O.S., 2 Vols, Vol. II, 1928, Baroda, p. 473.
31. K. Krishna Murthy, *Sculptures of Vajrayāna Buddhism*, 1989, Delhi, p. 46.
32. B. Bhattacharya (Ed), *Abhayakara Gupta's Niṣpannayōgavali*, GOS No.CIX, Baroda, 1949, p. 58.
33. B. Bhattacharya, *The Indian Buddhist Iconography*, Calcutta, 1968, p. 125-26.
34. K. Krishna Murthy, *Op.cit.*, 1989, p. 47.
35. S. Samasrami (Ed), *Karanda Vyuha*, Calcutta, pp. 21-22
36. K. Krishna Murthy, *Op. cit.*, 1989, p. 8.
37. *Ibid*, p. 47
38. Rhys Davids (Ed), *Thomas Watter's in Huan-Tsang travels in India*, Delhi, 1961, p. 215 and 224.
39. Alice Getty, *The Gods of Northern Buddhism*, Delhi, 1978, p. 59.
40. A. Rea, 'Explorations and Excavations of ancient sites' *ARASI*, Calcutta, 1908-09, pp. 1-10.
41. *Ibid.*, p. 6.
42. Senart (Ed), *Mahāvāstu* Vol. I, p. 253.
43. Rhys Davids (Ed), *Op.cit.*, 1961, Vol.II, p. 216.

44. K. Krishna Murty, *Op.cit.,* 1989, p. 53.
45. N.K. Bhattasali, *Iconography of Buddhist and Brāhmanical sculptures in the Decca Museum*, Delhi, 1972, p. 87.
46. *Ibid.,* p. 86.
47. Waddell, 'Evolution of Buddhist cult; its Gods, images and Art', *The Imperial and Asiatic Quarterly Review*, January, 1912, p. 148 and Alice Getty, *Op.cit.*, 1978, p. 86.
48. *Ibid.,* p. 146.
49. Krishna Sastry V.V., Proto and Early historic cultures of A.P., 1983, Hyderabad, p. 186.
50. Author's personal discovery. Now it is preserved in Visakha Museum, Visakhaptnam.
51. N.K. Bhattasali, *Op. cit.,* 1972, p. 63.
52. Alice Getty, *Op. cit.,*1978, p. 86.
53. Sir Aurel Stein, *Report of the Archaeological Society of India*, Frontier Circle, London, 1911-12, p. 8.
54. L.K. Srinivasan, 'Some medieval sculptures from Ratnal District, Meerut', *Śrī Ramachandrika*, New Delhi, 1993, pp. 319-330.
55. D. Hanumantha Rao, 'A unique sculpture of Gaṇapati from Sankaram' *Śrī Ramachandrika* (Ed), I.K. Sarma and A.V.N. Murthy, New Delhi, 1993, pp. 347-50.
56. B. Bhattacharya (Ed), *Op.cit.,* 1928, pp. 592-93.
57. B. Bhattacharya, *Op.cit.,* 1949, p. 62.
58. *Ibid.,* p. 72.
59. I.K. Sarma, 'Unique *uṣṇīṣa* (coping stone) from Amaravati, *Śrī Mallampalli Somasekhara Sarma, Commemoration volume*, pp. 279-284.
60. B. Bhattacharya, *Op.cit.,* p. 292, Fig. 190; p. 291, Fig. 189.
61. *I.A.R.*, 1963-64, p. 12 & 107.
62. *E.I.,* Vol. XXXVI, pp. 227-74.
63. V.V. Krishna Sastry, *Three grants of Pṛithvī Śrī Mūla Rāja from Kondavidu*, Hyderabad, 1992, pp. 2-3.
64. K. Rama, *Buddhist art of Nagarjunakonda*, New Delhi, 1995, p. 44.
65. *E.I.,* Vol. XXXIV, p. 210.
66. N. Ramesan, Copper plate inscriptions of Andhra Pradesh Govt. Museuem, No. I, Hyderabad 1962, p. 36.
67. *A.R.A.S.I.,* Calcutta 1907-08, p. 164, Fig. 8.
68. V.V. Krishna Sastry, *Op.cit.,* p. 86.
69. K. Raghavachary 'Dharaṇikōṭa' and its western contacts' *Q.R.H.S.*, XII, No. 3, Calcutta, 1972-73, pp. 167-68.
70. *Luder's* list 1, 225 & 271 and also P.V.P. Sastry, 1987, p. 45.
71. *Ibid.,* p. 45.
72. Rhys Davids (Ed), *Op.cit.,* 1961, p. 214-215.

73. *E.I.*, Vol. X, pp. 43-44 & S.I, pp. 25-28.
74. *E.I.*, Vol.VI, p. 155.
75. *Ibid.*, p. 159.
76. *Epigraphia Zeylanica,* IV, 1943, p. 90
77. Referred by B.S.L. Hanumantha Rao, *'Dhānyakaṭaka in Early Andhra History'* (*in making of* Andhra History), 1987, p. 11.
78. P.V.P. Sastry, 'Andhra desa Charitralo Dharaṇikōṭa' Dhānyakaṭaka (*in making of Andhra History*), Guntur, 1987 p. 58.
79. P.R.K. Prasad, 'Amareswaralaya Prachineeta'—A Review, *Dhānyakaṭaka (in making of Andhra History)* Guntur, 1987, p. 61.
80. *I.A.R,* 1973-74, pp. 4-5.
81. T.N. Ramachandran, *The Nagapattinam and other Buddhist Bronzes in the Madras Museum*, Bulletin of the Madras Government Museum, 1965, Vol.VII, No. 1, pp. 63-64, Plate XXII (1) to (4).
82. Excavations at Nelakondapalli, Khammam district' (unpublished report), Bronze Icon is now displayed in B.S.A. Museum, Guntur.
83. Indian Antiquary, Vol. I, p. 153.
84. O.C. Gangooly, *Andhra Sculpture*, Hyderabad 1973, p. 83 and also see ARASI, 1926-27, p. 153.
85. B. Bhattacharya (Ed), *Op.cit.*, 1928, p.
86. Hariprasad Sastri, *Advaya Vajra—Advaya Vajra Saṅgraha*, G.O.S, No. XL, Baroda, 1927, pp. 40-41.
87. B. Bhattacharya, *Op.cit.*, 1949, p. 5.
88. N.K. Bhattasali, *Op.cit.*, 1972, pp. 30-31.
89. *Ibid.*, pl. X.
90. Alice Getty, *Op.cit.*, 1978, p. 30.
91. *E.I,* XXV, p. 19.
92. B. Bhattacharya, *Op.cit.*, 1928, p. 56.
93. B. Bhattacharya (Ed), *Op.cit.*, 1949, p. 50.
94. *Ibid.*, p. 66.
95. B. Bhattacharya (Ed), *Op.cit.*, 1928, p. 49.
96. Alice Getty, *Op.cit.*, 1978, p. 22.
97. S. Beal, *Buddhist records of western world, translated from the Chinese of Hiuen Tsang*, London, 1906, p. 134.
98. K. Krishna Murthy, *Op.cit.*, 1989, p. 24.
99. T.N. Ramachandran, *op.cit.*, p. 52.
100. *The Vajrasādhana Tantra*, p. 24, referred by K. Krishna Murthy, *in sculptures of Vajrayāna Buddhism*, 1989, p. 25.
101. B. Bhattacharya (Ed), *Op.cit.*, 1928, p. 473.
102. N.K. Bhattasali, *Op.cit.*, 1972, pp. 36-37.
103. B. Bhattacharya, *Op.cit.*, 1968, pp. 156-64.

104. B. Bhattacharya (Ed), *Op.cit.,* 1928, p .88.
105. *Ibid.,* p.176.
106. B. Bhattacharya, *Op.cit.,* 1968, p. 227.
107. Alice Getly, *Op.cit.,* 1978, pp. 123-24.
108. *Ibid.,* pp.125-26.
109. B. Bhattacharya (Ed), *Op.cit.,* 1928, p. 210.
110. Referred by B.Bhattacharya in *The Indian Buddhist Iconography*, 1968, p. 190.
111. *I.A.R.,* 1958-59, p. 5, Pls. IB.
112. B. Bhattacharya (Ed), *Op. cit.,* 1928, p. 564.
113. N.K. Bhattasali, *Op.cit.,* 1972, p. 35.
114. Alice Getty, *Op.cit.,* 1978, p. 159.
115. *I.A.R.,* 1958-59, p. 5.
116. Alice Getty, *Op.cit.,* 1978, p. 160.
117. B. Bhattacharya, *Op.cit.,* 1968, p. 238.
118. *Ibid.,* p. 238.
119. Alice Getty, *Op.cit.,* 1978, p. 160.
120. P.R. Ramachandra Rao, *Andhra Sculpture,* 1984, Pl LXII, Fig. 172.
121. *Ibid.*, Pl. LXIII, Fig. 193.
122. *Ibid.*, Pl. XC, Fig. 266.
123. Presently displayed in B.S.A.Museum at Guntur.
124. T.N. Ramachandran, Buddhist Sculptures from a stūpa near Goli village, Guntur district, B.M.G.M. Madras, 1929, Pl. IX, p. 16.
125. R. Subrahmanyam, *Salihundam - A Buddhist site in Andhra Pradesh*, Hyderabad, 1964, p. XLIV.
126. *Ibid.,* p. 85.
127. *E.I.,* Vol. XXVIII, pp. 135-36.
128. *E.I.,* Vol. XXVII, pp. 133ff.
129. *ARASI,* 1919-20, pp. 35ff.
130. R. Subrahmanyam, *Op.cit.,* pp. 83-90.
131. *JAHRS*, Vol.XXIX, Parts 3 & 4, p. 24.
132. *ARASI*, 1919-20, p. 36.
133. *Ibid.,* p. 37.
134. Alice Getty, *Op.cit.,* 1978, p. 132.
135. D.C. Bhattacharya, *Op. cit.,* 1978, p. 21.
136. *ARASI*, 1919-20, p. 36.
137. D.C. Bhattacharya, *Op.cit.,* 1978, p. 22.
138. B. Bhattacharya, *Op.cit.,* 1968, p. 209.
139. D.C. Bhattacharya, *Op.cit.,* 1978, p. 21.
140. Alice Getty, *Op.cit.,* 1978, p. 134.
141. *Ibid.,* p.134.

142. D.C. Bhattacharya, *Op.cit.,* 1978, p. 20.
143. Alice Getty, *Op.cit.,* 1978, p. XLI, Fig. a.
144. W.E. Clark, Two Lamaistic Pantheons, 2 Vols., Cambridge Mass, 1937, Fig. No. 6B 2-92, p. 207.
145. D.C. Bhattacharya, *Op.cit.,* 1978, Pl. 9, p. 22.
146. Gordon, Iconography of Tibetan Lamaim, New York, 1939, Fig. 1, p. 74, and see Alice Getty, the Gods of Northern Buddhism, 1978, pl. XXXIX b.
147. B. Bhattacharya, *Op.cit.,* 1928, p. 134.
148. *ARASI,* 1919-20, p. 38.
149. K. Krishna Murthy, *Op.cit.,* 1989, pp. 38-39.
150. B. Bhattacharya, *Op.cit.,* 1928, p. 105.
151. Gordon, *Op.cit.,* 1939, p. 68.
152. B. Bhattacharya, *Op.cit.,* 1968, p. 117.
153. *ARASI,* 1919-20, p. 38.
154. K. Krishna Murthy, *Op.cit.,* 1989, p. 40.
155. B. Bhattacharya, *Op.cit.,* 1928, pp. 39-41.
156. N.K. Bhattisali, *Op.cit.,* 1972, pp. 25-26, pl. VII a.
157. Gordon, *Op.cit.,* 1939, p. 66.
158. *ARASI,* 1919-20, p. 38.
159. *JESI*, Vol.VII, pp. 67-68.
160. I.K. Sarma, Studies in Early Buddhist monuments and Brahmi inscriptions of Āndhradēśa, Nagapur, 1988, p. 82.
161. Srinivas Ritti, 'Buddhism in Kannada inscriptions', *Ratna Chandrika* (Panorama of Oriental Studies) Ed. Devendra Handa & Ashvini Agrawal, Delhi, 1989, p. 318.
162. N.K. Bhattasali, *Op.cit.,* 1972, p. 58.
163. Alice Gettey, *Op.cit.,* 1978, pp. 120-21.
164. D.C. Bhattacharya, *Op.cit.,* 1978, p. 13.
165. *Ibid.,* p. 13.
166. Haraprasad Shastri (Ed), *Op.cit.,* 1927, p. 43.
167. Debala Mitra, *Buddhist Monuments*, Calcutta, 1971, p. 193.
168. *Ibid.,* p. 193.
169. I.K. Sarma, 'Archaeological Evidences pertaining to Buddhism in Tamilnadu' *Śrī Rama Chandrika*, Ed. A.V.N. Murthy and I.K. Sarma, Delhi, 1993, pp. 65-77.
170. *ARASI,* 1919-20, p. 38.
171. B. Bhattacharya, *Op.cit.,* 1928, p. 215.
172. Alice Getty, *Op.cit.,* 1978, p. 122.
173. K. Krishna Murthy, *Mirrors of Indian Culture*, Delhi, 1982, pp. 132-33.
174. *Ibid.*, p. 132.
175. *ARAD*, 1926-27, pp. 155-56.

176. *ARASI*, 1919-20, pp. 37-38.
177. *Ibid.*, p. 38.
178. *ARASI*, 1919-20, p. 38.
179. Alice Getty, *Op.cit.*, 1978, p. 110.
180. B. Bhattacharya, *Op.cit.*, 1968, pp. 94-95.
181. Alice Getty, *Op.cit.*, 1978, pp. 110-114.
182. B. Bhattacharya, *Op.cit.*, 19768, pp. 100-101.
183. B. Bhattacharya (Ed), *Op.cit.*, 1928, p. 49.
184. B. Bhattacharya(Ed), *Op.cit.*, 1949, p. 48.
185. Alice Getty, *Op.cit.*, 1978, p. 113.
186. N.K. Bhattasali, *Op.cit.*, 1972, pp. 28-29.
187. B. Bhattacharya, *Op.cit.*, 1968, p. 102, Fig. 74.
188. Robert Sewell, List of Antiquarian Remains in Madras Presidency, Vol. I, London, 1883, pp. 35-36.
189. A. Rea, G.O. No.646, *STBA* (1894) Pl. IV, Govt. of Madras.
190. *I.A.R.*, 1916-62, p. 97 & also see *I.A.R.*, 1968-69, p. 64.
191. I.K. Sarma, *Op.cit.*, 1988, p. 85.
192. *I.A.R*, 1976-77, p. 74.
193. *ARASI*, 1919-20, p. 38.
194. *JESI*, Vol. VII, pp. 67-68.
195. Srinivas Ritti, *Op.cit.*, 1989, p. 318.
196. N.K. Bhattasali, *Op.cit.*, 1972, p. 58.
197. Alice Getty, *Op.cit.*, 1978, p. 68.
198. *Ibid.*, p. 61.
199. T.N. Ramachandran, 'Nagarjunakonda', *M.A.S.I*, 1938, p. 71.
200. *ARAD.*, 1926-27, pp. 155-56.
201. O.C. Gangooly, *Andhra Sculpture*, Hyderabad, 1973, p. 83 and also see *JAHS*, 1928, pl. I and *ARASI,* 1926-27, p. 153.
202. Debala Mitra, *Op.cit.*, 1971, p. 228.
203. *Ibid.*, p. 113.
204. *E.I.*, XXVI, 1941-42, pp. 171 ff.
205. Inspected and examined by the author. The image is locally worshipped as *Bujjeswara* and *Buddheswara.*
206. Debala Mitra, *Op.cit.*, 1971, pp. 190-97.
207. Personal discovery of the author near Kollapatu in the island of Pulicat.
208. Hara Prasad Shastri (Ed), *Op.cit.*, 1927, p. 41.
209. Gordon, *Op.cit.*, 1939, p. 27.
210. *IAR*, 1961-62, p. 3.
211. *IAR*, 1957-58, p. 64.
212. The sculptures are reported for the first time by the author who visited the site in the month of April 1999.

213. B. Bhattacharya (Ed), *Op.cit.,* 1928, p. 394.
214. Alice Getty, *Op.cit.,* 1978, p. 135.
215. *Ibid.*, p. 135.
216. B. Bhattacharya, *Op.cit.,* 1978, p. 215, pl. 277.
217. The sculpture is presently displayed in V.J. Museum, Vijayawada, A.P.
218. Alice Getty, *Op.cit.,* 1978, p. 11.
210. *MASI*, 1910-11, pp. 77-80.
220. Personal communication from I.K. Sarma (Superintendent (Retd.)) who shifted the sculptures from Ramatirtham to Salihundam for their safety.
221. Reported by K. Sai Bhakta Kesava (TA) Nellore. The image is now displayed at the district archaeological museum, Nellore.
222. The image is personally examined and identified as Amitābha by the author. Presently it is available in the village.
223. Marg, Vol.XXXIX, No. 4, p. 72.
224. Nandadeva Wijesekara (Ed), *Sculpture* (Archaeological dept. centenary 1890-1990, commorative series, Vol. IV, pp. 48-50, Fig. in pp. 113, 90, 87.
225. Hara Prasad Sastri (Ed), *Op.cit.*, 1927, p. 41.
226. *IAR,* 1974-75, p. 2.
227. Reported by Dr. E. Siva Nagi Reddy (D.M.) and later it was examined and identified, Buddha as Akṣobhya by the author.
228. *IAR*, 1973-75, pp. 4-5.
229. *ARASI*, 1919-20, pp. 37-38.
230. Hara Prasad Sastri (Ed), *Op.cit.*, 1927, pp. 40-41.
231. Presently displayed in Bauddha Sri Archaeological Museum, Guntur. It was examined by the author and identified Buddha as Bodhisattva Padmapāṇi.
232. T.N. Ramachandran, *op.cit.,* 1929, Pl. IX, p. 16.
233. S. Paranavitana, *The stūpa in Ceylon*, M.A.S. Ceylon, Vol. V, Colombo, 1947, Pl. IX.
234. *Journal of the Royal Asiatic Society*, London, 1895, p. 617.
235. *Indian Antiquary*, Vol. I, p. 153.
236. T.N. Ramachandran, *Op.cit.,* 1965, Pl. XXII, Fig. 4.
237. D.L.N. Sastry, Excavations at Nelakondapalli, unpublished report, 1999, (A & M, Hyderabad).
238. Now it is in Baudha Sri Archaeological Museum, Guntur. On stylistic grounds it is dated to post-Gupta period.
239. Alice Getty, *Op.cit.,* 1978, p. 61.
240. *Ibid.,* p. 61.

## TAMILNADU

Buddhism in Tamilnadu enjoyed a longer spell, right from the early centuries of Christian era till late medieval periods. The reason for this appears to be the existence of several important port towns along the coast which perhaps facilitated not only trade and transportation but also religious propagation. The glorious epoch of this religion was well recorded in ancient Tamil literature i.e. *Manimekālai* and *Silappadikaram*. It is true that the Mauryan emperor Aśōka, introduced the religion in this land through his missionaries under the leadership of Mahēndra in Tondaimaṇḍalam and also in other parts of Tamil country.[1] The occurrence of Buddhist names like Tavīra (monk) and Matavīrai (nun) in early Brahmi characters (2nd c.B.C.) engraved in the cave inscriptions of Tamil Nadu, clearly suggests that the early entry of Buddhism in this region even prior to Aśōkan times.[2]

The *Mahāvaṁsa* mentions that the king Duttagamini (101-77 B.C.) invited the monks and kings from this region to witness the construction of the *mahāstūpa* in Śrīlanka.[3] The Nagarjunakonda inscription of Śrī Mādhariputra Vīrapuriṣadatta (3rd c.A.D.) mentions certain territories in the South, including 'Damila'. Scholars identified 'Damila' with Tamil country.[4] A copper plate grant of Sundara Chōla, father of Rāja Rāja (1006 A.D.) refers to the donation of land to a Buddhist temple.[5] *Mattavilāsa Prahāsana* of the Pallava king Mahendravarman (600-30 A.D.) describes the conditions of the monasteries and monks of this region.[6] This is also attested by the Chinese traveller Hieun-Tsang.[7] During this period, the port-towns of Kanchipuram, Kaveripattinam and Nagapattinam flourished as trade centres on the coast which helped religious propagation.

Some localities like Kama Kottamatha near the Kamaksiamman temple, Vaikuntha Perumal, Ekambreswara temple, Pallavamedu, Jnana Prakasa Svanugalmatha etc. at Kanchipuram yielded several Buddhist remains. The excavations at Kamaksiamman temple brought to light vestiges of *stūpas*, *chaityas* and *vihāras* besides few copper coins belonging to Rudra Sātakarṇi, coin moulds and *Buddhapāda* slabs, datable from 1st B.C. to 4th c. A.D.[8] Several Buddha images of a later date (9th c. A.D.) were also unearthed. Among them are the interesting seated images of Buddha in *vīrāsana* posture in *dhyāna mudrā*, another seated on lotus in *yōga mudrā* and an image in *bhūmisparśa mudrā*.[9] Several images including the *Mahāparinirvāṇa* scene belonging to the late medieval period, were found in the niches on the compound wall of the Ekamabreswara temple.[10] According to a Korean inscription (1378 A.D.) an Indian monk namely Dhyānabhadra heard an illuminating lecture by a Buddhist teacher at Kanchipuram. The Kalyani inscription at Zaingganaing (Burma) of Dhammacheti (1472-92 A.D.) mentions an Ananda *Thera*, a native of Kanchipuram[11], who was well versed in the *Tripīṭakas*, visited Pugama (Pagan) in Burma.[12]

Excavations at Kaveripattinam yielded remains of a brick built Buddhist *vihāra*, datable to 2nd-3rd c.A.D. At Pallavaneswaram, a *stūpa* (6th c.A.D.) decorated with stucco work was noticed. Associated with the brick structures were an image of a seated Buddha in *dhyāna mudrā,* a lime stone slab depicting *Buddhapāda* and few stucco figures.[13]

The principal port town—Nagapattanam, was a trade centre from where images of Buddha and Buddhist panels, carved in stone and metal were exported to the different parts of south India and also to other South-east Asian countries. It was a famous emporium during Chōla times, especially for casting bronze images of Buddha and other Brāhmanical icons. Several bronze images of Buddha of Vajrayāna faith were unearthed from the ruins of a monastic establishment datable to the Chōla period (pl. 14 & 15). A Buddhist temple was constructed exclusively for the Chinese monks during the rule of Pallava King Narasimha Varman II (695-722 A.D.)[14] The Sailendra king Mara Vijayottunga Varma of Sumatra built a *vihāra* called Chuḍāmaṇi Varma *Vihāra* in memory of his father, as known from the larger Leiden Plates (1006 A.D.)[15] The Kalyani inscription (1476 A.D.) of Dhammacheti, king of Pegu refers to the visit of the monks to Padarikārāma monastery and worship of Buddha under the instructions of the Chinese rule.[16] The multi-storeyed Pagoda (30 mtrs. high) reported by Walter Elliot in 1846 at Nagapattanam serves as a classical example for non-Indian Buddhist monument constructed for the benefit of Chinese monks during the period of the ruler Xian Chun in 1267 A.D.[17]

The discovery of several images and icons of Buddha from different parts of the State such as Tiruvatti (South Arcot Dist.), Pallur, Kanikiluppai (North Arcot), Manganallur, Elaiyur, Perunjeru, Tiruvalanjuli, Melaiyur, Pallisvaram, Kattapadi, Kaveripattanam (Tanjore dist.), Sathanmalli Vellanore, Pugalur (Tiruchy dist.), Alangudipatti, Vellanallur (Pudukkottai dist.), Tyaganur (Salem dist.), Karur and Jayankonda Cholapuram (Tiruchirapalli dist.), Kuvam (Chengleput dist.), Manikandi (Ramanathapuram dist.) etc. suggest that though Buddhism entered Tamil Nadu in Aśōkan times, it existed upto the post-Vijayanagara or Nayaka period.

In Tamilnadu, the Vājrayāna phase of Buddhism is also characterised by the presence of icons and images with prominent flaming *uṣṇiṣa* and *uṇna* and also Buddhist creed formulae inscribed on the pedestals.

## MELAIYUR

A beautiful image of gold plated icon (copper gilt) of Maitreya (39.5 cm. height) was reported as treasure trove in the year 1927 at Melaiyur near Tiruval, the place of Tirumangai Alwar in the Shiyali taluk - 45 kms. from Nagapattanam in Tanjore district. (Now in Boston Museum).

**Maitrēya :** It is a rare example to be reported from South India not only in the delineation of form, ornaments and drapery but also in the history of bronze gilding. He is shown standing in *samabhaṅga* on a circular lotus pedestal (39.5 cms. height). Both the hands are found missing. Well decorated *karaṇḍamakuṭa* (head gear) with an effigy of *stūpa* and *uṛna* on the forehead are important features to identify the icon as Maitrēya (Pl. 51). Eyes were inlaid with silver.[18] *Makara kuṇḍalas*, *śiraścakra* and a broad necklace with pendants, a garland like *yajñōpavīta*, a thick under garment with lines, tassels, loops and securing strings arranged in elegant knots are some of the characteristic iconographical features that not only reflect the features of the Pallava and Rashtrakuta schools of art but also tally with the images of Nalanda and Kurkihar datable to 9th c.A.D. The icon stands as a classical example in the bronze art tradition of South India. Probably it is the earliest of all the Buddhist bronzes of Tamil Nadu so far reported.[19] The icon appears to be one of the original attendant figures of the Buddha (Front cover page) found at Nagapattanam.[20]

## TYAGNUR

It is in Attur taluk of Salem district. Two figures were reported from this village, one in a modern temple and the other in a field nearby the village.

a) **Buddha in *Dhyāna mudrā* :** It is carved in granite stone kept in a temple. He is shown seated in *padmāsana* on a pedestal in *dhyāna mudrā*. It is a highly developed form of the Buddha with an unfinished *uṣṇīṣa* which was left uncarved as a lump (Pl.52). The square face, the prominent nose, the full lips, the strong and broad shoulders, the highly proportionate limbs and torso which make the image a perfect and magnificent specimen of a developed form. It is similar to the late Buddha images reported from Amaravati. On stylistic grounds, it is dated to 10th c.A.D.[21]

b) **Buddha :** It is also similar to the above one in all iconographical details. His facial expression is suggestive of joy borne out of love and compassion (Pl. 52a). The oval face, uṣṇīṣa and other features suggest the influence of South East Asian School of art. It is dated to 11th-12th c.A.D.

## MADAGARAM

It is small village in Tanjore district. A figure of Buddha was reported from this village and later on shifted to the Art Gallery, Tanjore.[22]

**Buddha (Amitābha) :** Buddha seated in *padmāsana* shows well worked details such as the curls of hair, the *ur̩na,* the *civara* and the lower garment on the legs. The square face and the *trivali* on the neck clearly indicate the late Chōla art datable to 10th c.A.D. The expression of the face shows the sublime bliss and suggestiveness of grace. The Buddha in *dhyāna mudrā* is worshipped in the name of Amitābha and a *dhyāna* for his worship is mentioned in *Advaya Vajra Saṅgraha.*[23]

## ELAIYUR

A sculpture of Buddha was reported from this village located in Tanjore district. It is carved in granite stone and datable to 11th c.A.D.

**Buddha (Amitābha) :** He is shown seated on a *padmāsana* in *dhyāna mudrā*. The *trivali* on the neck and elongated *uṣṇīṣa* on the cranium are prominently shown (Pl. 53). The oval face, the lips, the nose, squarish shoulders are some of the peculiar features which represent the influence of foreign art traditions. The disproportionate iconometry of the figure gives a fairly late date i.e. 16th c.A.D.[24]

## MANAMBADY

It is also a small village situated in Tanjore taluk. A sculpture of Buddha carved in granite stone was reported from this village.

**Buddha in *dhyāna mudrā* :** He is seated in a decorated *bhadrāsana*. A semi circular halo with *makaras* at either end above the shoulders is neatly delineated (Pl. 54). The oval face and slender shoulders suggest the influence of indegenous art tradition.[25] On stylistic grounds, it is dated to 12th c.A.D. Similar images were reported from Kollapattu in Nellore district of Andhra Pradesh.[26]

## TANJORE

A standing Buddha icon (105.5 cm.) in bronze (Pl. 54a) and a stone image were reported from Tanjore city which later on shifted to Madras Museum.

**Buddha :** Elegantly moulded it shows Buddha standing in *samabhaṅga* attitude with ornamental *prabhāvaḷi* supported by a *makara tōraṇa* surmounted by *kirtimukha* (Pl. 55). He is represented in *abhaya* and *varada mudrā* with palm marks. *Ur̩na* is marked in the shape of Brahmi letter '*tha*' or '*ya*'. The long robe with folded edges was wrapped over the body like the Roman *toga* leaving the right chest and arm bare and covering an under garment. The *uṣṇīṣa* is shaped like fire in five flames. The oval face, bored ear lobes, pointed nose, highly ornated *prabhāvaḷi* suggest a late date i.e. Vijayanagara period.[27]

## TIRUVATTI

A seated Buddha was reported from this village in south Arcot district. It was carved in granite stone and dated to 11th c.A.D. on stylistic grounds.

**Buddha (Amitābha) :** The sculpture though slightly disfigured, it retains all the iconographical features intact. He is shown seated in *padmāsana* on a pedestal in *Dhyāna mudrā*. The *uṣṇīṣa* is well worked-out like a flame which rises directly from the cranium itself. The curls of hair, the *civaras*, the torso and facial expressions indicate of sublime tranquility (Pl. 56). The elongated ear lobes, smiling face, the lips, oval face, snubbed nose, suggest the influence of South Asian School of Art.[28] A *Dhyāna* for his worship is mentioned in *Advaya Vajra Saṅgraha*.[29]

## JAYANNA KONDA CHOLAPURAM

Few sculptures of Buddha in *dhyāna mudrā* (Pl. 57a, b & c) were reported from this place, in Tiruchirapalli district. One of the images was installed on a tank called Paluppurani (in Tamil it means 'one who is ripe'). The image was carved in granite stone and datable to 11-12th c.A.D.[30]

**Buddha in *Dhyāna mudrā* :** Amitābha is shown as usual in *padmāsana*. The iconographical details such as the curls of hair, the flame over the cranium, the *civaras*, the *trivali* and the depression on the neck are prominently seen (Pl. 57c). It is well modelled and endowed with great spiritual potentialities. The subtle smiling face and the powerful and broad shoulders suggest the influence of foreign tradition. The important feature of the figure is the depiction of oval shaped halo behind the head. Along the margin of the halo are carved three pronged flaming buds and on the top an umbrella with the branches of the Bodhi tree which probably suggest the royal status of Śākyasiṁha Buddha.

## KANCHIPURAM

The Tamil epic *Manimēkhalai* (550 A.D.) speaks of the prosperous condition of the Buddhist monasteries of the South. It mentions a *chaitya* erected in the middle of Kanchipuram to house a golden Bōdhi tree with emerald leaves and another shrine dedicated to Lord Buddha.[31] During the period between 7th-9th c. A.D., many Buddhist monks migrated from Kanchipuram to the monasteries of Apanka or Kurkihar in Bihar for taking shelter as there existed strong anti-Buddhist wave at Kanchipuram.[32] It was also attested by the discovery of several Buddhist icons found at Kurkihar in Bihar which contain inscriptions recording the gifts made by the monks who hailed from *Kanchidesa* or *Kanchimaṇḍaladesa.*[33]

Hieun Tsang, the Chinese traveller mentions that in the country of Chu-li-ya, the Buddhist monasteries were in ruins and there were several tens of *Deva* temples and the *Digambaras* were numerous. The picture of Draviḍa, with its capital at Kanchipuram was comparatively bright where the traveller noticed more than hundred monasteries with about 10,000 monks belonging to the Sthavīra School.[34]

It was during the reign of the Pallava king of Kanchipuram, the great Buddhist *Āchārya* called Vajrabodhi (661-730 A.D.) carried the tenets of Vajrayāna or Taṅtrayāna pantheon of Buddhism to China and Śrīvijaya.[35] In the holy city of Kanchipuram, in the precincts of the temples, on the walls of the temples and also at public places, several images of Buddha (Pl. 58, 59, 60a, b & c) were reported which range in date from 7th to 15th centuries A.D., which suggests that the site continued to exist as a prominent Buddhist centre in the Tamil country.

a) **Buddha (Akṣobhya) :** It was found in the Karukkilamarnda amman temple. The image (3'-9") is shown seated in *padmāsana* on an ornamental *pīṭha* in *bhūsparśa mudrā* (Pl. 58). The iconographical details closely resemble the images of Chōla type. Interestingly, the halo inside is beautifully delineated with tassels like a garland jetting out from the wide open mouths of *makaras* and flames on the outside margin. On styllistic grounds, it is dated to 11-12th c.A.D.[36]

b) **Buddha (Amitābha) :** This sculpture (2'-6") also comes from the same temple complex mentioned above. Except for the depiction of *prabhāvaḷi*, the facial features and the other iconographical details are found to be one and the same as found in the above. Here the *prabhāvaḷi* is supported by pilasters carved on either side with *yali* or lion bases and *makaras* ejecting garlands from their wide open mouths on the top of the abacus of the pilasters.[37] The *uṣṇīṣa* is shown as a tongue of flame which looks like a feather of peacock on the cranium (Pl. 60b). On stylistic grounds, it is dated to 13th-14th c.A.D. It is iconographically similar to the one reported from Nagapattanam.[38]

c) **Buddha in *Dhyāna mudrā* :** This sculpture was noticed near the Police Station in Śiva Kanchipuram (Pl. 60c). He is seated in *padmāsana* on a double lotus pedestal. It is carved very meticulously, delineating features like *trivali* at the neck and flaming *uṣṇīṣa*. The oval face, the lips, the elongated nose and eyebrows suggest the influence of South East Asian School of Art. On stylistic grounds, it is dated to 11-12th c.A.D.[39]

## NAGAPATTANAM

It was an important port town located in two sea routes from India to China. It was variously known as Nikama (Ptolemy)[40], Nagavadana (I-tsing) and Pa-tan (Marcopolo). For the first time a Kalyāni Chālukyan inscription of Dhammacēti (1476 A.D.) calls this place as Navutapaṭṭaṇa.[41] It was indeed a major centre of Buddhism that produced casting Buddhist bronzes right from 9th c.A.D. and continued to produce such beautiful images upto 17th c.A.D. The icons reported from this place are more elegant which emphasize the stately repose and contemplative form of the Buddha. There was a setback for Buddhists during 7th-9th c.A.D. from the Brāhmanical saints particularly from the Vaishnavites. The Vaishnava saint Tirumangai raided a Buddhist temple at Nagapattanam and carried an icon of Buddha made in gold and he melted it down and used the same for decorating the Viṣṇu temple at Śrīrangam.[42] Since the days of the Chōlas (871-1250 A.D.), Nagapattanam existed as a place of pilgrimage for Mālaya Buddhists. It was Śrīvijaya dynasty that supported the declining Buddhism by constructing Buddhist temples at Nagapattanam (11th-12th c.A.D.).[43]

In 1856, four bronze icons and a porcelain image of Buddha were recovered from a brick chamber near ancient tower called Puduveli Gopuram or Chinese pagoda in Nagapattanam.[44] Important ones are taken up for study.

a) **Buddha :** He is shown standing in *samabhaṅga* with *abhaya* and *varada mudrās* and flaming *uṣṇīṣa*. The inscription on the pedestal of the image reads '*Svasti Śrī Agama paṇḍitarāi vyyakkonda Nayatanar*'. It means "Hail prosperity! The Nayakar (Buddha) who assured the salvation of scholarly *paṇḍits* who learnt the *Agama (Nikāya* which is *Suttapīṭaka)*." He is shown with prominent flaming *uṣṇīṣa*. The *Saṅghati* is a long cloth in wavy lines covering from neck to toes.[45]

b) **Buddha in *Bhūsparśa mudrā* :** He is seated in *vajraparyaṅkāsana* on a lotus pedestal in *bhūsparśa mudrā*. An aureole of flames surmounted by the Bōdhi tree is very meticulously depicted. The delineation of folds of the robe, elongation and perforation of the ear lobes, low chin and drawn forward open eyes and beholding hair in stud like curls surmounted by a high flame like *uṣṇīṣa,* circular *uṛna*, a full blown lotus mark on the left palm and the sole of right foot and the arrangement of under garment folds in front of his crossed legs clearly suggest the features of Vijayanagara school of Art.[46]

**Buddha :** Buddha standing (73.5 cm. height) on a lotus pedestal is attached to a *siṁhāsana*. The right hand is in *abhaya* while the left hand isin *kaṭaka mudrā* devoid of palm marks. No *uṛna* mark is seen on the forehead. These are seven rows of conventionalised curls of hair surmounted by the *uṣṇīṣa* in five flames (Pl. 61). The delineation of feet, hands, fingers, bored ear lobes, facial features and torso obviously suggest the indegenous art of South India datable to Early Chola period (10th c.A.D.)[47]

**Buddha :** It is similar to the above. The pedestal base has an illegible inscription in Tamil characters (12-13th c.A.D.) which reads "*Potta*" (Buddha) probably a donor's name and '*Nayakar*' i.e. the Lord. The image of Buddha which is the object of offering. He is represented in *abhaya* and *varada mudrās* with palm marks. *Uṛna* is shown like a hook with a tang. Nose is long and acquiline. Ear lobes are long and bored. Adorned with seven rows of curly hair studs surmounted by a flame like *uṣṇīṣa*.[48]

Diggings in localities known as Velippalayam and Nanayakkara street in Nagapattanam in the year 1926 and 1934 brought to light nearly 350 Buddhist bronze items. They chronologically range in date from Chōla to Vijayanagara or Nāyaka period.[49] Some of the bronzes are available in the Museum on Fine Arts in Boston, Madras Govt. Museum, Madras, A.P. State Museum, Hyderabad. etc.

**Seated Buddha :** A beautiful bronze icon (60 × 39 cms.) of Buddha with silver inlay is shown seated on a richly ornamented throne (now it is in Fine Arts Museum, Boston)[50]. He sits in the *padmāsana* with the left hand on his lap in the *dhyāna mudrā* and the other raised in the *vyākhyāna mudrā* (Pl. 62). Over the series of small curls of hair covering his head, is a flame tipped *uṣṇīṣa*. A profusely decorated fragile screen serves as a backdrop for the Buddha. The throne is decorated with *Gajakēsari* motifs at either end. Above his head is a separate piece and a delicate canopy surmounted with fanciful, stylised foliage with *makaras* supported by pilasters. On the rear of the throne at either end are hooks along its lower edge, meant for keeping two attendant images probably of the Bōdhisattvas namely Avalōkitēśvara and Maitrēya. A gilt bronze Maitrēya found at Melaiyur, seems to be one of the original figure attending upon this Buddha. He is dressed in royal attire and visualized as crowned and bejewelled. The figure has a socket beneath its hollow pedestal which seems to fit the hooks on the rear of the throne. Maitrēya's eyes were also inlaid with silver.

**Buddha in *Bhūsparśa mudrā* :** It was reported from Velippalayam (1926). He is shown seated on a lotus pedestal in *bhūsparśa mudrā* (20.7 cms. height). The soles of the feet and left hand bear the marks of the Sun with emanating rays within a diamond shaped enclosure. *Uṛna* is marked in a hook with bifurcated tang. Elongated ears with holes, bent down face, with drawn chin, *uṣṇīṣa* with tongue of flames shown like a lotus bud are some of the peculiar features, commonly seen in the images reported from Burma.[51] A *dhyāna* is prescribed in the *Advayavajra Saṅgraha* for his worship.[52]

**Buddha (Akşobhya) :** It is also similar to the above one. The lotus pedestal is inscribed with a label inscription reads as '*Udaiyar*' which refers to the Buddha himself. The mark on the left palm is shown with full blown lotus within a diamond shaped enclosure whereas the *uṛna* is shown as a circle. The face is round and the long ears are bored (Pl. 63). The flaming *uṣṇīṣa* has a ruby in front.[53] The iconographical features are more akin to the Buddha figures reported from Kanchipuram.[54] A *dhyāna* for his worship is mentioned in the *Niṣpannayōgāvaḷi.*[55]

**Buddha in *dhyāna mudrā (Amitābha)* :** It is from Nanayakkara street of Nagapattanam. He is shown seated on a lotus pedestal over a *bhadrāsana* which adorned with lions (Pl. 63a). The aureole is depicted with arched border and the *Bōdhi* tree, the leaves of which are arranged in a semi circular pattern.[56] This type of flaming *uṣṇīṣa* and the absence of bored ear lobes suggest the close affinity with the images reported from Kanchipuram.[57] The palm mark on the upper left hand is shown with a dot in a circle in a diamond shape enclosure whereas *uṛna* in an elongated hook with a pointed tang.

**Buddha *(Amitābha)*** : Amitābha is shown in *Dhyāna mudrā* seated on a lotus pedestal on an elevated *siṁhāsana* with a back rest (73 cms. height). The outer edge of aureole is prominently shown with flames which is surmounted by an umbrella and finally covered by a semi-circular plate incised with rich foliage (Pl. 64). A pair of Nāgarājas holding *cāmara dhāris* at either end behind a throne with their right hands in *vismaya* pose, suggest that they are singing in praise of the God.[58]

**Avalōkitēśvara :** Four armed Avalōkitēśvara is shown standing in *tribhaṅga* on a circular lotus pedestal (14.4 cm. height), holding a rosary and a *kundika* (vase) in the upper right and left hands, the lower right hand is in *varada* while the left with a lotus. He is decorated with *makarakuṇḍalas*, necklace, *yajñōpavīta*, waist girdle, armlets, wristlets, *śiriscakra*. *Uṛna* is marked with a dot. A diamond shape mark with a vertical line on the left lower line is the palm mark of the lower right hand. He wears an ornamental *jaṭāmakuṭa*. The general iconographical features of the deity is perfectly modelled. The image represents the form of *Jaṭāmakuṭa*

Lōkēśvara which is one of the forms of Avalōkitēśvara.[59] Early icons of Avalōkitēśvara were reported from Nelakondapalli[60], Amaravati[61] and images from Gummadidurru[62] and Ramathirtham[63] in Andhra Pradesh.

The other image which represented with four hands (Pl. 65) holds in the upper right hand a rosary and the lower hand raised in pose of exposition (*vyākhyāna* or *vitarka mudrā*) whereas the upper left hand holds a blue lotus and the lower left hand is in *varada mudrā*.[64] The image is comparable with the images found at Kurkihar in Bihar.[65]

Another image which is in *tribhaṅga* posture shown standing on a circular lotus pedestal with elaborate *prabhāvaḷi* (105 cms.). He is represented with four hands. The upper right hand holds a rosary and left hand with the stalk of a lotus and crowned by a group of flowers whereas the lower right hand is in *abhaya* and the corresponding left hand is in *varada mudrā*. He is heavily ornamented with jewels. *Kirīṭamakuṭa* shows the figure of the *Dhyāni* Buddha Amitābha. The long pointed nose, dress and other features look so modern and it may be dated to the post-Vijayanagara times (Pl. 65a).

**Maitrēya :** This Standing image on a lotus pedestal in *tribhaṅga* (29 cms. height) on an elevated circular *padma pīṭha* is represented with four arms. The upper right hand holds a rosary and the left hand is broken (probably holds lotus) while the lower right hand is in *abhaya* and the left hand in *varada mudrā* with palm marks. Each palm mark is shown a dot in circle within a diamond shape enclosure and an arrow without tang on four corners. He is decorated with *kirita makuta, makara kuṇḍalas*, necklaces, three stranded *yajnopavīta*, waist girdle and tassels, armlets, wristlets, rings, *padasaras* and *śiraścakra* (Pl. 66). A miniature *stūpa* representation in *kirita makuta* helps to identify the icon as Maitrēya. A label inscription on the pedestal in Tamil characters reads '*Tiruvudaiyar ammai A Kālankai perumal*'. It means "the great being Akālanka, who is both mother and father of the World". On stylistic grounds, it is dated to 14th-15th c.A.D.[66] Early images of Maitrēya were reported from Amaravati[67] and Salihundam[68] in Andhra Pradesh, Ratnagiri in Orissa and Ellora in Maharashtra.[69]

The second image of Maitrēya is also shown standing on a circular lotus pedestal (20 cms. height) over a *bhadrāsana*. He is represented with two hands, the right hand is in *abhaya mudrā* with a palm mark while the left hand with the stalk of a flower. He is decked in ornaments and jewels. The *kirīṭamakuṭa* is shown with a figure of *stūpa* in front. The depiction of two stranded *yajñōpavīta,* necklaces, underware with design of a flower, *śiraścakra* and other iconographical features, suggests the late Chōla features.

The other image of Maitrēya shown standing (75 cms. height) on a lotus pedestal is repesented with four hands. The upper right hand holds a rosary and the left hand a flower from which spring ten flowers and two buds whereas the lower right hand is in *varada* and the left hand is in *kaṭaka mudrā* with palm marks. The *stūpa* on the *jaṭāmakuṭa* is prominently shown (Pl. 67). On stylistic grounds, it is dated to 10th c. A.D. A *dhyāna* is mentioned in the *Sādhanamāla.*[70]

**Ṣaḍakṣari Lōkēśvara :** He is seated on a lotus pedestal in *vajraparyaṅkāsana* and represented with four hands. The upper right and left hands hold a rosary and lotus respectively whereas the lower hands in *añjali* attitude. The *Dhyāni* Buddha Amitābha is figured on the *jaṭāmakuṭa* (Pl. 68). He is decked in all ornaments and jewels. The undergarment is extended upto the ankles. On stylistic grounds, it is dated to the early Chōla times.[71]

When Lōkēśvara is associated with the great knowledge of the six syllables he is called Ṣaḍakṣari Lōkēśvara. There are four *Sādhanās* mentioned in the *Sādhanamāla.* Except one form, in all the three, he is accompanied by Ṣaḍakṣari Mahāvidya. The *dhyāna* for his worship is given as follows :[72]

*Atmanam Lōkēśvararupam Sarvalankara bhuṣitaṁ suklavarnam vamatah padmadharam daksnato 'ksausutradharam aparabhyam hastabhyam hrdi samputanjalisthitam dhyayat. Dakṣiṇe Manidharam tatta dvarnabhujanvitam padmanatroparistham. Vame thataiva apara padma stham sadaksarim Mahāvidyam.*

'The worshipper should think himself as Ṣaḍakṣari. Lōkēśvara who is decked in all sorts of ornaments, white in colour and four armed carrying the lotus in the left hand and the rosary in the right. The other two hands are joined in forming the *mudrā* of clasped hand against the chest. To his right is Manidhara in similar colour with same pose sitting on a lotus. To the left is Ṣaḍakṣari Mahāvidya with identical form sitting on another lotus.'

Images of Ṣaḍakṣari group are reported from Sarnath and Indian Museums.[73]

**Padmapāṇi :** Though the iconographical features of the image (7.7 cms. height) are similar to the above one, it differs in holding the attributes. The delineation of *karaṇḍa makuta* with pyramidal design, *patrakuṇḍalas, channavīra*, waist gridle, *śiraśchakra*, undergarment, necklaces, armlets etc. suggests the influence of Javanese school of art (Pl. 69). His right hand extended upto its elbow resting on the right knee while the left hand rests on the seat and holding the stalk of a blue lotus, seen clearly at the shoulder level.[74] On stylistic grounds, it is datable to 11th c.A.D. Images of *Padmapāṇi* were also reported from Amaravati[75], Nelakondapalli[76], Salihundam[77] in Andhra Pradesh.

**Khadiravani Tārā :** She is seated in the *lalitāsana* on an oval lotus pedestal (13 cms. height) and represented with two hands. The right hand is in *varada mudrā* while the left hand with the *utpala* or blue lotus (Pl. 70). The hands are shown with palm marks. She is decked in ornaments and jewels. She wears a prominent head gear. On stylistic grounds, it is dated to late Chōḷa period.[78] A *dhyāna* is prescribed in the *Sādhanamāla* for her worship.[79] An image of this type was reported from Amaravati in Andhra Pradesh.[80]

**Tārā:** Standing on a circular lotus pedestal (10.2 cms. height), her right hand is shown in *varada mudrā* while the left hand with the stalk of a lotus (*utpala*) as if it is issuing from the lotus pedestal (Pl. 70a). *Uṛna* is shown on the forehead as a dot. The depiction of ornaments and other iconographical features, clearly indicate the influence of Gāndhāra School of Art.[81] Images of Tārā were reported from Amaravati[82] and Salihundam[83] in Andhra Pradesh.

**Lōkēśvara :** He is shown seated in the *Mahārāja lilāsana* on a pedestal. (10.3 cm. height). He represents *kaṭaka mudrā* with his right hand and the left hand rests on the pedestal (Pl. 71). The conical head gear, *yajñōpavīta* made out of deer skin, wristlets, rings for the thumb, *pādasaras* etc. are shown prominently. Undergarment extends upto the ankles. *Jaṭāmakuṭa* with its frontal decorative design is defaced. Iconographically, the features correspond to the stone images of late Pallava period (9th c.A.D.) He is a favourite deity to the Mahāyanists who cures all diseases.[84] He is one of the important emanations of *dhyāni* Buddha Amitābha.[85]

**Jambhala :** He is shown seated in the *lalitāsana* on a circular lotus pedestal (10.5 cms. height). Her right hand holds a citron while the left hand carries a mongoose (Pl. 72). The depiction of head gear, *makara kuṇḍalas*, necklaces, waist girdle around the pot belly, three stranded *yajñōpavīta*, armlets, anklets, *śiraścakra*, undergarment etc. suggests the influence of the Gāndhāra School of Art. On stylistic grounds, it is dated to Early Chola times.[86] Interestingly, an early image of Jambhala in stucco was reported from the excavations at Amaravati in Andhra Pradesh[87] and also stone sculptures from Orissa and Sarnath.[88] A *sādhana* for his worship is mentioned in the *Sādhanamāla*.[89]

**Jambhala and Vasudhara :** They are shown seated on long oval lotus pedestal (10 cms. height) in the *lalita* pose (Pl. 73). His right hand holds a citron while the left with the mongoose. The animal here represents the receptacle of all gems and jewels, so that when it pressed by the Jambhala it vomits forth riches which are collected in bags of money. To his left is seated Vasudhara in *lalitāsana*. Her left leg which hangs down kicks bag of riches. Her right hand holds a cup of jewels, probably to shower on devotees and her left hand with the ear of corn. She is decked in all ornaments and jewels. On stylistic grounds, it is dated to early Chōla times.[90]

**Buddha (Amitābha) :** An early sculpture of Buddha (2 mts. high) datable to 9th c.A.D. was reported from Nagapattanam region. (displayed in the Brooklyn Museum) (Pl. 63c). He is shown seated under the Bōdhi tree on a *siṁhāsana.*[91] An oval shaped aureole, a *chatravali,* the cushion which was placed against the throne back, the tree, the flying Bōdhisattvas, flaming *uṣṇīṣa,* etc. are some of the features which closely resemble with the sculptures of the Buddha reported from Jayanakonda Cholapuram.[92]

### MANIKANDI

It is a small village in Ramanathapuram district. A sculpture of Buddha carved in granite was reported from the village which is dated on styllistic grounds to 13th c.A.D.

**Buddha :** He is shown seated on a lotus pedestal in *vajra paryaṅkāsana.* The aureole and the flaming *uṣṇīṣa* were fully developed (Pl. 74). Though it is mutilated, the features remain expresses the sublime peace. An illegible inscription in *Grantha* script on the pedestal of the image suggests that it is the only inscribed sculpture reported from Tamil Nadu region so far.[93]

### KUVAM

It is a small village in Chengalput district. A figure of Buddha was reported from this village and later on shifted to Madras Museum. On stylistic grounds, it is dated to 13th c.A.D.

**Buddha as Amitābha:** It is a well carved image in granite stone which looks like images reported from Kanchipuram. Interestingly, the image is encompassed by a decorated *prabhāvaḷi* supported by *makaras* (Pl. 75). Feather like *uṣṇīṣa,* depiction of ear lobes and facial features suggest the influence of South East Asian art tradition.[94]

## PONDICHERRY

From the Union territory of Pondicherry, altogether two images of Buddha were reported from (a) Arikamedu (Kakayan tope or Mound of Jina)[95], south of Pondicherry and (b) Karadikkuppam, north of Pondicherry.[96]

a) **Buddha in *Dhyāna mudrā* :** He is seated in *Dhyāna mudrā* on a pedestal. The features such as three garments, the curls of hair, *uṣṇīṣa* and *trivali* on the neck are very meticulously delineated. The *prabhāvaḷi* in the form of a *makara tōraṇa* behind the head and the flaming *uṣṇīṣa* on the cranium are the prominent features which added beauty to the sculpture to look more elegant (Pl. 76). Similar examples were reported from Kollapattu and Kunthur in Nellore district of Andhra Pradesh. On stylistic grounds, it is dated to the post Chōla times.

b) **Buddha in *Dhyāna mudrā* :** It is also similar to the above one in all iconographical features. Interestingly the *uṣṇīṣa* is shown in five tongued flame with a base (Pl. 77). The *prabhāvaḷi*, in the shape of *makara tōraṇa* with cusped design at its outer edge is an other interesting feature of the sculpture. On stylistic grounds, it is dated to 12th c.A.D.

Thus, the widespread of Buddhism in Tamil country is well attested by the discovery of a range of stone images, brick structures, epigraphs, several life-size images besides numerous bronze icons from a variety of sites located in the districts of Tanjore, Trichnopaly and Nagapattanam. Nagapattanam was the principle coastal town which produced Buddhist bronzes from 9th c.A.D. to 17th c.A.D. From here the icons belonging to Vajrayāna phase of Buddhism were transported to other parts of India and also to South East Asian countries.

## REFERENCES

1. R. Sathiantha Iyer, *Studies in Ancient History of Tondaimaṇḍalam*, Madras, 1944, p. 45.
2. I.K. Sarma, 'Archaeological Evidences pertaining to Buddhism in Tamil Nadu' in *Rama Chandrika,* Ed. A.V.N. Murthy and I.K. Sarma, Delhi, 1993, p. 66.
3. *Ibid.*, p. 66.
4. *E.I.*, XX, pp. 7 & 22.
5. I.K. Sarma, *Op.cit.*, 1993, p. 67.
6. Michael Lock Wood and Vishnu Bhatt, *Mattavilasa Prahasana,* Madras, 1981, pp. 43-45.
7. Rhys Davids, *Thomas Watter's on Yuan Chwang Travels*, Part II, 1961, p. 26.
8. *I.A.R.*, 1962-63, p. 12.
9. T.A. Gopinatha Rao, 'Budha vestiges in Kanchipura', in *I.A.*, 1915, pp. 127-29.
10. Debala Mitra, *Op.cit.*, 1971, p. 194.
11. *Ibid.*, p. 194.
12. *I.A.*, XXII, 1893, p. 29.
13. K.S.Ramachandran, *Archaeology of South India,* Tamil Nadu, 1980, pp. 123-26 and *IAR,* 1969, pp. 24-25.
14. T.N.Ramachandran, *The Nagapattanam and other Bronzes in Madras Museum,* Bulletin of the Madras Museum, New Series, General Section, Vol. II, No. 1, Madras, 1956, p. 14.

15. D.C. Sarkar, *Select Inscriptions,* Vol. II, Delhi, 1983, pp. 620-21.
16. *I.A.*, Vol. XXII, 1893, p. 29.
17. *I.A.*, Vol. VII, 1878, p. 224.
18. A. Aiyyappan and P.R. Srinivasan, *Story of Buddhism with special reference to South India,* Madras, 1960, pp. 79-80.
19. T.N. Ramachandran, *Op.cit.,* 1965, pp. 56-57.
20. Vidya Dehija, 'The persistence of Buddhism in Tamilnadu', *Marg,* Vol. XXXIX, No. IV, p .65.
21. A. Aiyyappan and P.R. Srinivasan, *Op.cit.,* 1960, p. 93.
22. *Ibid.,* p. 93.
23. Haraprasad Sastri (ed.) *Advayavajra Saṅgraha,* GOS No. XL, Baroda, 1927, pp. 49-50.
24. A. Aiyyappan and P.R. Srinivasan, *Op.cit.,* 1960, p. 95.
25. *Ibid.,* p. 98.
26. Reported by Sri K. Sai Bhakta Kesava, Technical Assistant, Nellore, and later examined by the author.
27. A. Aiyyappan and P.R. Srinivasan, *Op.cit.,* 1960, p. 95.
28. *Ibid.,* p. 93.
29. Haraprasada Sastri, ed., *Op.cit.,* 1927, pp. 49-50.
30. A. Aiyyappan and P.R. Srinivasan, *Op.cit.,* 1960, p. 94, fig. 25.
31. Michael Lockwood and Vishnu Bhatt, *Op.cit.,* 1981, pp. 43-45.
32. T.A. Gopinatha Rao, '*Buddha Vestiges in Kanchipura*' *Indian Antiquary,* 1915, pp. 127-29.
33. Vidya Dehijia, *Op.cit.,* Marg, Vol. XXXIX, No. 4, p. 58.
34. Rhys Davids, *Op.cit.,* 1905, p. 226.
35. A. Aiyyappan and P.R. Srinivasan, *Op.cit.,* 1916, p. 61.
36. *Ibid.,* p. 98, fig. 29.
37. *Ibid.,* p. 99, fig. 30.
38. Vidya Dehijia, *Marg,* Vol. XXXIX, No. 4, p. 71.
39. Debala Mitra, *Op.cit.,* 1971, p. 194, Pl. 122.
40. *I.A.*, Vol. XIII, p. 332.
41. *I.A.*, Vol. XXII, pp. 11-53.
42. Vidya Dehijia, *Marg,* Vol. XXXIX, No. 4, p. 58.
43. T.N.Ramachandran, *Op.cit.,* 1965, pp. 16-17.
44. Indian Antiquary, Vol. VII, pp. 224-27.
45. T.N.Ramachandran, *Op.cit.,* 1965, pp. 23-24.
46. *Ibid.,* p. 24.
47. *Ibid.,* p. 43, pl. V, fig. 2.
48. *Ibid.,* p. 43, pl. V, fig. 2.
49. Vidya Dehijia, *Marg,* Vol. XXXIX, No. 4, p. 60.
50. *Ibid.,* p. 60.
51. T.N. Ramachandran, *Op.cit.,* 1965, p. 45.

52. Hara Prasad Sastri (ed.) *Op.cit.*, 1927, pp. 51-52.
53. T.N. Ramachandran, *Op.cit.*, 1965, p. 45, pl. II, fig. 2.
54. *I.A.*, Vol. XLIV, pp. 127-29.
55. B.Bhattacharya, ed. *Abhayakara Gupta's— Niṣpannayōgavali, GOS,* No. CIX, Baroda, 1949, p. 5.
56. T.N. Ramachandran, *Op.cit.*, 1965, p. 51, pl. XII, fig. 5.
57. *I.A.*, Vol. XLIV, pp. 127-29.
58. T.N.Ramachandran, *Op.cit.*, 1965, p. 42, pl. VII, fig. 1.
59. *Ibid.*, p. 51, pl. VII, fig. 1.
60. D.L.N. Sastry, *Excavations at Nelakondapalli,* Unpublished Report 1999, Archaeology & Museums, Hyderabad. The icon is now displayed in B.S.A. Museum, Guntur.
61. P.R. Ramachandra Rao, *Andhra Sculpture,* Hyderabad, 1984, Pl. LXVIII, fig. 194.
62. *ARAD,* 1926-27, pp. 156-57.
63. K. Krishnamurthy, *Sculptures of Vajrayāna Buddhism,* Delhi, 1989, p. 46.
64. T.N. Ramachandran, *Op.cit.*, 1965, p. 52, pl. VII, fig. 2.
65. Debala Mitra, *Op.cit.*, 1971, pp. 89-90.
66. T.N. Ramachandran, *Op.cit.*, 1965, p. 52, pl. VI, fig. 2.
67. K. Krishna Murthy, *Op.cit.*, 1989, p. 24.
68. *ARASI,* 1919-20, p. 36.
69. Debala Mitra, *Op.cit.*, 1971, pp. 225-31 and 184.
70. B.Bhattacharya, ed. *Op.cit.*, 1971, p. 49.
71. T.N.Ramachandran, *Op.cit.*, 1965, p.57.
72. B. Bhattacharya, *Op.cit.*, 1928, p. 27.
73. B. Bhattacharya, *Op.cit.*, 1968, pp. 125-27.
74. T.N. Ramachandran, *Op.cit.*, 1965, p. 57.
75. K. Krishnamurthy, *Op.cit.*, 1989, pp. 23-24.
76. *ARASI,* 1919-20, p. 36.
77. D.L.N. Sastry, *Excavations at Nelakondapalli,* Unpublished Report 1999, Archaeology & Museums, Hyderabad.
78. T.N. Ramachandran, *Op.cit.*, 1965, p. 58.
79. B. Bhattacharya, ed. *Op.cit.*, 1928, p. 176.
80. K. Krishna Murthy, *Op.cit.*, 1989, p. 28.
81. T.N.Ramachandran, *Op.cit.*, 1965, p. 58.
82. K. Krishna Murthy, *Op.cit.*, 1989, pp. 27-28.
83. *ARASI,* 1919-20, pp. 35-36.
84. T.N. Ramachandran, *Op.cit.*, 1965, p. 54.
85. B. Bhattacharya, *Op.cit.*, 1958, p. 124.
84. P.N. Ramachandran, *Op.cit.*, 1965, p. 54.
85. B. Bhattacharya, *Op.cit.*, 1968, p. 124.

86. T.N. Ramachandran, *Op.cit.*, 1965, p. 58.
87. K. Krishnamurthy, *Mirrors of Indian Culture*, Delhi, 1982, pp. 134-35, pl. XIII.
88. Debala Mitra, *Op.cit.*, 1971, p. 68.
89. B. Bhattacharya, *Op.cit.*, 1928, p. 564.
90. T.N. Ramachandran, *Op.cit.*, 1965, p. 59.
91. Vidya Dehijia, *Marg*, Vol. XXXIX, No. IV, p. 74, pl. XVIII.
92. A. Aiyyappan and P.R. Srinivasan, *Op.cit.*, 1960, fig. 25.
93. *Ibid.*, p. 100.
94. *Ibid.*, p. 98.
95. A. Ramaswamy, *History of Pondicherry*, Delhi, 1987, p. 15.
96. A. Aiyyappan and P.R. Srinivasan, *Op.cit.*, 1960, pp. 91-92.

# KARNATAKA

Aśōkan Rock edicts found at various places such as Maski, Gavimath, Palkigundu, Brahmagiri, Jatinga-Rameswara and Siddapur suggest that Aśōka was instrumental in spreading Buddhism in the Karnaṭaka region. The discovery of a brick *chaityagṛiha,* near the Minor rock edict of Aśōka at Brahmagiri, may be the earliest Buddhist structural evidence in support of the above view.[1]

In the early centuries of Christian era, Vanavāsi was the cradle for Buddhism as known from various inscriptions and other cultural materials. An Ikṣvāku inscription from Nagarjunakonda mentions that Taṁbapaṇṇika Thēriyas visited Kāśmīra, Gāṅdhāra and other regions and countries including Vanavāsi, (*Kāśmīra-Gāṅdhāra-Chīna-Chilāta-Tōsali-Aavanta-Vaṅga-Vanavāsiya vana-Damila-Pālura-Taṁbhapaṇṇi-dupapasāda Kānam Thēriyanam Thaṁbapannakānāṁ Supari gahe)*[2]. Kodabalisiri, the queen of the King of Vanavāsi and the sister of the king Ehuvala Chaṁtamūla, donated a *chaitya* with a four winged monastery to the monks of the *Mahiśāsaka* sect at Nagarjunakonda.[3] The inscription from Vanavāsi belonging to the Chutu king Viṇhukaḍa Chuṭukulananda Sātakarṇi speaks of the flourishing conditions of Buddhism and also the construction of a *vihāra* for the monks by the Queen Śivaskanda Nāgasiri, the daughter of the Chūṭu king.[4] A *śrēṣṭhi* (merchant) by name Bhūtapāla of Vanavāsi caused the construction of a Śilāgṛiha of Kārla (*Vējayantitō Sēthinō Bhūtapālēna Śilāghāram parinithapitaṁ Jaṁbūdvīpasi utamām*) which was considered at one time the best *ārāma* in the *Jaṁbūdvīpa.*[5]

The *āyaka* pillar inscription from the Vanavasi refers to Śivaśrī Pulumāvi who erected a *chhāyāstaṁbha*, in memory of the Sātavāhana queen.[6] A fragmentary Brahmi label inscription reading '*Tārāsa pulusa dānaṁ*' from Hampi ruins refers to the donation by an individual.[7] The occurrence of broken pillars and other fragments in the complex of Hampi clearly suggests the existence of Buddhism in the early centuries of Christian era in Karnataka region.

Another important Buddhist site is Sannati, belonging to the Sātavāhana period located on the banks of the river Bhima. Excavations brought to light vestiges of *stūpas*, brick structures, sculptured panels, early historic pottery, N.B.P. ware, Brahmi label inscriptions, coins, beads, bangles, terracotta tiles, sculptures, Buddhapāda slabs and memorial stones which reflect the material culture of the Sātavāhanas.[8] The Sanskrit inscriptions from this region stand as testimony to the hold of Sātavāhanas and Mahāraṭhis, besides a host of other officers like *Rājamātya* and house-holders who contributed their mite to the establishment and development of the monastic complex at Sannati.[9] Recent excavations at Kanganahalli near Sannati brought to light several inscriptions from the *Stūpa* area which refer to the names of the kings with their portraits. Images of the Buddha in standing and sitting postures, *āyaka sthaṁbas*, slabs depicted with *Jataka* stories and numerous Sātavāhana coins are some of the other findings. The most outstanding discovery from the site is a slab carved with figures of the Mauryan king Aśōka and his wife, flanked by attendants. Interestingly, a label inscription beneath the slab in Brāhmi characters reads as *Rāya Aśōko*. It is for the first time to notice a portrait of an emperor Aśōka as far as the Indian Art History is concerned.[10]

The Kadaṁbas (4th-5th c.A.D.) who succeeded the Sātavāhanas were basically Saivites. However, the Halsi plates of Kadaṁba king Ravivarma refer to the *Śramana Saṅgha*. The copper plates of the Bhōja king Aśaṅkita, issued from Hiregutti (Kumta Tq.) dated to 6th century A.D. mention the Buddha (*aparimita-gaṇa-guṇa-nidhi and nishkarama-Vatsala)* and certain donations made to the Buddhist monastery.[11]

During the medieval period, the Chālukyas of Kalyāna (11-12th c.A.D.) had extended their support to Buddhism. The inscriptions from Balligave (Shimoga district), Dambal and Koliwad (Dharwad District) refers to the construction of *vihāras* and installation of icons of Tārā Bhagavati for worship. The Shikarpur inscription (1065 A.D.) speaks of the establishment of the Jayanti Prabudha *vihāra* at Balligave (Belgam district) and made donations for the *vihāra* and also for the worship of Tārā, Lōkēśvara and Buddha.[12] The inscription dated to 1098 A.D. refers to a Buddhist worshipper by name Nagiyaka, who installed an image Tārā in Belgam region.[13] The Tumkur inscription (1151 A.D.) invokes the universal spirit of Jina who is Śiva, Dhatri, Sugata (Buddha) and Viṣṇu. The Chiknayakahalli inscription (1181 A.D.) praises Ballāladeva as a supporter of the followers of Mahēśvara, Buddha, Viṣṇu and Arhat.[14] The *Vihāras* at Kadarika near Mangalore in South Kanara district, housed bronzes of Buddha, Bōdhisattvas and three headed and six armed Lōkēśvara. The label inscription (10th c.A.D.) on the bronze icon of Lōkēśvara mentions the name of the king of Alupa who installed the icon in the *vihāra*.[15] Thus, though Buddhism entered the Karnataka area a couple of centuries preceding the Christian era, it continued to flourish only upto the medieval times that too at a few places. In Karnataka the Vajrayāna phase of Buddhism is represented by the presence of images and icons and Buddhist creed formulae inscribed on the pedestal of the images.

## MANGALORE

Scholars are of the opinion that the famous temple at Mangalaṁbika at Mangalore and Mukaṁbika near Coondapur might have been originally Buddhist in character. Same is the case with the famous Mañjunātha temple at Kadri near Mangalore. The rock cut caves nearby the village Kadri, indicate the Buddhist affiliation to this place. The discovery of bronze icons of Buddha, Lokēśwara, Hālāhala Lōkēśvara in Mañjunātha temple complex, obviously suggests that the present temple dedicated to Śiva as Mañjunātha was originally a temple dedicated to Mañjuśrī a familiar deity in *Mahāyāna* or *Vajrayāna* pantheon of Buddhism.[16] Of the three bronzes, the sixed armed Hālāhala Lōkēśvara stands as a masterpiece in Chōla art tradition prevalent in the area.

***Dhyāni* Buddha (Amitābha) :** Buddha seated in *padmāsana* (2 ft. high) with his right hand held in *vyakhyāna mudrā* and his left hand on the lap with palm facing upwards is an important image (Pl. 78). The oval face, the nose, the lips and the fine garment suggest the influence of South East Asian art tradition. The elaborate *uṣṇīṣa* with flame of fire is depicted boldly when compared to the other Buddha images reported from Nagapaṭṭanam. The facial expression is unmistakably vigorous. The suggestive masculine strength rather than feminine tenderness with which Buddha images are commonly endowed, effects the benign qualities of the Buddha. A *dhyāna* for his worship is mentioned in the *Advaya Vajra Saṅgraha*.[17]

**Lōkanātha :** He is shown seated in *dhyāna* on a *pīṭha* with four hands. He wears a well worked *jaṭāmukuṭa* decorated with a *pushpāvali* and a *maṇipaṭṭa* at its base with an effigy of the *Dhyāni* Buddha Amitābha in a circle in front. He has a third eye on the forehead The *makarakuṇḍalas* in the ears are decorated with a flower on their tops. He is well ornated with jewels. The *yajñōpavīta* is of deer skin indicated by the deer head on it found on the left portion of the chest (Pl. 79). The waist band of jewels has a finely wrought *siṁha mukha* clasp. The two upper hands are in the *kaṭaka mudrā* and the lower right hand is in *varada mudrā* bearing probably a *ratna* or *maṇi* and while the lower left hand is in the *vyākhyāna mudrā*.[18] Out of four *sādhanās* described to the worship of Lōkanātha, only one *Sādhana* describes him as accompanied by Tārā and Hayagṛīva and other eight Bōdhisattvas and also four goddesses. The *sādhana* which is applicable to Lōkanātha under study is as follows :[19]

*Pūrvavat-kramayogena Lokanāthaṁ śaśīprabhaṁ*
*Hriḥkārākṣarasambhūtaṁ jaṭāmukuṭa maṇḍitaṁ*
*Vajradharmajaṭantaḥsthaṁ aśeṣaroganāśanaṁ*
*Varadaṁ dakṣiṇe haste vāme padmadharaṁ tathā*

*Lalitākṣepasaṁsthaṁ tu mahāsaumyaṁ prabhāsvaraṁ*
*Varadotpalakarā saumyā Tārā dakṣiṇataḥ sthitā*
*Vandanā daṇḍaahastastu Hayagṛivo'tha Vāmataḥ*
*Raktavarno Mahāraudro vyāghracarmāmbarapriyaḥ.*

'The worshipper should think himself as Lōkanātha, resplendent like the moon, as springing from the sacred syllable *Hrīh* and wearing the *jaṭāmukuṭa*. He has within his matted hair the figure of the god, Vajradharma, the destroyer of all diseases, exhibits the *varada mudrā* and the right hand and carries the lotus in the left. Setting in *Lalitāsana*, is peaceful and resplendent. To his right is Tārā, who has a peaceful appearance, exhibits the *varada mudrā* and carries the lotus. To the left is Hayagṛīva, who displays the gesture of bowing and carries the staff in his two hands. He is red in colour, appears terrible and is clad in the garment of tiger-skin.'

Another *sādhana* adds an account of the deities constituting the Lōkanātha Maṇḍala, including the Bōdhisattvas and the gate-keepers. The *dhyāna* is given as follows :[20]

*Tadvaratakāṣtadale padme Maitreyādiṁ ca vinyaset*
*Maitrēyaḥ pītavarnaśca nāgapuspavarapradaḥ*
*Kṣitigarbhaḥ śyāmavarṇaḥ kalaśaṁ cābhayaṁ tathā*
*Vajrapāṇiśca śuklābho vajrahasto varapradaḥ*
*Khagarbho nabhaḥsyāmabho cintāmaṇi varapradaḥ*
*Mañjughoṣaḥ kanakābhaḥ khaḍgapustakadhārakaḥ*
*Gaganagañjo raktavarṇo nīlōtpalavarapradaḥ*
*Viṣkambhī tu kṣāravarṇo ratnottamavarapradaḥ*
*Sāmantabhadraḥ pitābhaḥ ratnotpalavārapragāḥ*
*Dhūpādicaturddevī ca Vajrānkusyādidvaragah*
*Varnāyudhe yathāpurvaṁ Maṇḍalasyānusārataḥ*
*Evamvidaiḥ samāyuktaṁ Lokanāthaṁ prabhāvayet*

'On the eight petals of the lotus should be placed the gods Maitrēya and others. Maitrēya is yellow in colour, carries the Nāga (kēsara) flower and exhibits the *varada* pose. Kṣitigarbha is of green colour, carries the *kalaśa* and exhibits the *abhaya* pose. Vajrapāṇi is whitish in colour, carries the *vajra* and exhibits the *abhaya mudrā*. Khagarbha has the colour of the blue sky, carries the *Cintāmaṇi* and exhibits the *varada mudrā*. Mañjughoṣa is of golden complexion and carries in his two hands the sword and the book. Gaganagrñja is of red colour, carries the lotus and exhibits the *varada mudrā*. Viṣkambhin is ash-coloured, carries the excellent jewel and exhibits the *varada mudrā*. Sāmantabhadra is yellowish in complexion, carries the jewel on a lotus and exhibits the *varada mudrā*. The four goddesses Dhūpā and others accompany Lōkanātha and the four goddesses Vajrānkusi and others guard the gates, their colour and weapons being in accordance with the canons of the *Maṇḍala*. In this way Lōkanātha should be meditated upon by the worshipper.'

Though the *dhyānas* mentioned in the texts may not correspond to the iconographical details of the icon under-study particularly in the absence of holding *padma* in his hand, it is quite nearer to the first *dhyāna* described above. According to the *dhyānas* he is shown in the *lalita*, the *paryaṅka* or the *vajra paryaṅka* attitude. Similar type of images reported from Sarnath[21] and also icons from Mahoba[22], Baroda Museum[23] and Śrīnagar Museum.[24]

**Hālāhala Lōkēśvara :** This is the biggest and most interesting icon (4 ft. high) locally worshipped as Brahma. He is shown seated in *dhyāna mudrā* on a *padmāsana* over a *bhadrāsana*. He has three faces and six arms. The *jaṭāmakuṭa* is beautifully culled out and carries an effigy of the *Dhyāni* Buddha Amitābha in front. There is a flower above each ear. He is well ornamented with jewels. The *kēyūras*, armlets, rings to fingers and toes are very meticulously delineated. The *yajñōpavīta* in cloth is shown in exceedingly realistic fashion with the knot on the left chest (Pl. 80). All the three faces of the God have three eyes each and they are inlaid with silver leaves and small round black stones represent the pupils (Pl. 81).

The *bhadrāsana* has the stumps to support the aureole. On either end of the sunken portion of the *āsana* is a panel with seated figures in *añjali* (?) attended by a standing figure holding an unidentified object on either side. To the left side of the seated figure is a symbol, probably of a sword. The aureole has the usual flames on its outer edge and the tassels on its inner edge. At its top is a miniature pointed arched niche with a figure of Amitābha flanked by addorsed *makara* heads. The lower ends of the *prabhavali* are shown with creeper designs jetting out from the mouths of the *makaras*. Above each head of the *makara* is a standing figure of an attendant in *tribhaṅga* posture wearing *karaṇḍamakuṭa* and other ornaments. The left figure wears an *yajñōpavīta* and the right one a *vaikakṣa*. The hands of an attendant are in *kaṭaka* and *lōla* poses.[25]

Of the three right hands, the lower hand is in *varada mudrā* with a *ratna* or *maṇi*, the middle hand is in the *kaṭaka mudrā* and the upper hand holds a lotus bud while the lower left hand is in *vyākhyāna mudrā*, the middle one holds a lotus bud by its stalk and the upper hand is in *kaṭaka mudrā*. On the pedestal is the Sanskrit inscription in *Grantha* characters datable to 10th c. A.D. which mentions the name of the icon as Lōkēśvara caused to be engraved on it by the Alupa king Kundavarma. The inscription reads as follows :[26]

*Śrī Kundavarma gunavanatupēndra mahīpatiḥ*
*pādāravinda bramarō bālachandra sikhāmaniḥ*
*lokēśwarasya dēvasya pratisthāmikarō tprāhuḥ*
*śrīmat kadarika nāmni vihārē sumanohare*
*kalav vasa sahāsrānamatikrānte chatuṣṭayaṁ*
*punarabdhagate chaivasthashashtya samanvite*
*gateshu nava māseshu kanyāyam samsthiteguru*
*paschimevam rohinyam muhūrthe subhaka kshane*

'It means that the Alupa king Kundavarma installed a beautiful figure of the God Lōkēśvara in the pleasant *vihāra* at Kadri on the evening of that day in the month of i.e. *Makara,* in *Kali* 4068, which had *Rōhiṇi* as its star when Jupiter was in *Kanya* etc.'

The icon under study does not correspond to the *dhyānas* mentioned in the texts. The inscription on the icon clearly mentions the name of the figure as Lōkēśvara. Lōkēśvara or Bodisattva Avalōkitēśvara is one of the emanations of the *Dhyāni* Buddha Amitābha. Interestingly, the representation of an effigy of the parental *Dhyāni* Buddha Amitābha on the crown once again confirms that it is the form of Lōkēśvara. Hence there is no option except to look for a *Dhyāna* amongst the fourteen varieties of the Bōdhisattvas of this group. Out of four *Dhyānas*, the one that is applicable to this icon is as follows :[27]

*Hrīhkārabiījanispannaṁ Hālāhalam mahākṛpaṁ*
*Trinetraṁ trimukhaṁ caiva jaṭāmukuṭamaṇḍitaṁ*
*Prathamāsyaṁ sitaṁ niladakṣinaṁ vāmalohitaṁ*
*Śaśānkārdhadharaṁ mūrdhni kapālakṛtaswkharaṁ*
*Jatāntaḥsthajinaṁ saṁyak sarvābharaṇabhūṣitaṁ*
*Sitāravindanirbhāsaṁ śṛṅgārarasasundaraṁ*
*Ṣaḍbhujaṁ smeravaktraiṅ ca vyāghracarmambarapriyaṁ*
*Varadaṁ dakṣiṇe pāṇau dvitīye cāksamālikaṁ*
*Tṛtīye śaranarttanaṁ ca vāme cāpadharaṁ tathā*
*Dvitīye sitapadmaṁ ca tṛtīye stanameva ca*
*Vāmajānunā sitām Svābhadeviṁ dadhānaṁ.*
*Vāmena kamāladharāṁ dakṣiṇena bhujena*
*Bhagavadālinganaparaṁ kusumaśobhitājatakalāpaṁ.*
*Dakṣiṇapārsve sarpaveṣṭitaṁ triśūlaṁ, vamapārsve*

*padmasthakapālam nānāsugandhikusumaiaḥ sampūrnaṁ,*
*raktapadmacandre lilākṣepasthitaṁ vibhāvayet Bhagavantaṁ.*

'The worshipper should conceive himself as Hālahala, the great compassionate, originating from the sacred syllable *Hrīh* with three eyes, three faces and his matted hair rising upwards in the shape of a crown. The front (the principal) face is white, the right one is blue and the left is red. He bears on his head the crescent and the *kapāla*. The Jina Amitābha is with his matted hair and he is decked in all ornaments. He is resplendent like the white lotus and appears beautiful by the sentiment of passionate love he displays. He has six arms, with smiling face and wears garments of tiger skin. He displays the *varada mudrā* in the first right hand, the second has the rosary while the third flourishes the arrow. The first left hand carried the bow, the second the white lotus and the third touches the breast (of his *Śakti*). Śakti holds the lotus in the left hand and the right hand is engaged in the act of embracing the God. Her *jaṭa* is decorated with flowers. To their right is the trident entwined by a snake and on the left is the *kapāla* on the lotus, full of fragrant flowers. The God sits in the *Lalita* attitude on the red lotus.'

In one of the forms of Avalōkitēśvara, the six armed Hālāhala Lōkēśvara, holds a rosary, a lotus, a bow and an arrow. A trident encircled by a serpent to the right and a lotus supporting a skull filled with flowers to the left are prescribed. He is seated on a red lotus and holds his *Śakti* on his left knee, the right being stretched out. His colour is white.[28]

Though certain variations are observed between the *dhyāna* mentioned in the texts and iconographical details of the icon, in other aspects the icon is more or less satisfactorily answers the *Dhyāna*. Probably, he is the Buddhist counterpart of the image Vishapaharana of Saivite pantheon in respect of *mudrās*.[29]

This is the only bronze icon reported so far in India. Examples, more or less similar to this icon have been reported from Nepal.[30] Generally the iconographical features of Hālāhala is that he is accompanied by his Śakti or the female energy whom he carries on his lap. But the examples reported from Nepal and Kadri show that the God has been shown alone. This icon is more or less similar in conception to Sadaśivamurthi of Saivite pantheon.

## AIHOLE

Aihole, in Hindered taluk of Bijapur district is a famous Saivite pilgrim centre established by the kings of early Chālukyan dynasty during early medieval times. In the so-called two storeyed Jaina temple are identified some carvings of Buddhist affiliation, particularly of Mahāyāna phase.[31] Ther occurence of Mahāyāna Buddhist images such as a figure of seated Buddha on a boulder of the Meguti hill and an image of Avalōkītesvara from Badami (now displayed in the local museum) in the Chālukyan territory speaks the existence of Buddhist monastic complexes prior to the establishment of Chālukyan hegemony in these areas.

**Buddha in *Vyākhyāna mudrā* :** The storeyed rock-cut temple is an imposing structure generally known as Jaina *Basadi* (temple).[32] Each storey has a long spacious verandah with a frontage of four square pillars and two pilasters. On the back side of the upper storey is a rock cut room and three shrines. A figure of seated Buddha in *Vyākhyāna mudrā* is at the centre of the ceiling of the verandah with the upper garment and a prominent *Urṇa* on the forehead. Stylistically it is dated to the post Gupta times (6th century A.D.)

## KOLIVADA

From the village Kolivada in Hubli taluq of Dharwar district, an image of Tārā with an inscription on the pedestal was reported.[33]

**Tārā :** It is fairly well-preserved image seated in *lalitāsana* with two hands carved in granite stone. The inscription on the pedestal is in Nagari characters with the invocatory *'ye dharma hetu prabhāva'*. The image has some north Indian iconographical features. This is the last Buddhist vestige reported in Karnataka region which helps to take back the existence of Buddhism in the region to the late medieval times. Inscribed images with Buddhist creed formulae have also been reported from Kandhar in Maharashtra,[34] Amaravati[35] and Guntupalli[36] in Andhra Pradesh.

## BELAGAMI

A mutilated sculpture of Tārā-Bhagavati was reported from this village, located in Shikrapur taluq, Shimoga district.[37] One of the inscriptions dated 1065 A.D. from this place mentions about the construction of Jayanti prabha Bauddha *vihāra* by a *mahā pradhāna* called Rupabhattayya and also certain donations of land to the *vihāra* for not only worship of the idols installed by him namely Tārā-Bhagavati, Kēshavadēva, Lōkeśvaradēva and Bauddhadeva but also feeding to the *yōginis, kusalis* and *sanyāsis* (monks) residing in the *vihāra*.[38] Another inscription from the same place dated to 1067 A.D. refers to Nagiyaka, the wife of a faithful servant of the Chālukyan king, Trailōkayamalla who constructed a temple for Tārā-Bhagavati and granted some lands for its maintenance.[39]

**Tārā-Bhagavati :** The stone image (0.61 mt. high) though mutilated, retains the graceful and charming feature of the Goddess. Seated in *lalitāsana,* on a pedestal, she represents with two hands (Pl.82). Her charming face, half closed eyes, slender body and the posture obviously convey the important feature of the

Vajrayāna theology of *Karuna*. On stylistic grounds, it is dated to 11th c. A.D. It is one of the best specimens reported from South India. Tārā images were also reported from Amaravati[40] and Salihundam[41] in Andhra Pradesh and also Nagapaṭṭanam[42] in Tamilnadu.

Thus, discovery of Vajrayāna bronze icons and sculptures marks an important epoch not only in the history of Mahāyāna Buddhist tradition in Karnataka region but also suggests the continuation of the religion upto 10th c.A.D. Some of the iconographical features of the images found on the West Coast correspond to the Chōla images which may suggest the genetical link with the prosperous Buddhist centres located on the east coast.

## REFERENCES

1. Debala Mitra, *Buddhist Monuments*, Calcutta, 1971, p. 190.
2. *E.I.,* XX, p. 22 ff.
3. *Ibid.*, p. 24.
4. *E.I.,* XXXIV, pp. 238 ff.
5. S. Nagaraju, *Buddhist Architecture of Western India,* Delhi, 1986, p. 336.
6. A.V. Narasimha Murthy and Raghunath Bhat, *J.E.S.I.*, Vol. I, pp. 34 ff.
7. Srinivas Ritti, 'Buddhism in Kannada inscriptions' in Devendra Handa and Ashvini Agrawal, *Ratna Chandrika*, New Delhi, 1989, p. 317.
8. P.B. Desai, 'A new Buddhist centre' in the Journal of the Karnataka University, (Social Sciences), Vol. IV, 1968, pp. 158 ff.
9. *Q.J.M.S.*, Vol. LVI, 1965-66.
10. D.Jitender Das, "*Influence of Andhra-Buddhism in Northern Karnataka*" a paper submitted at the National Seminar on *Buddhist Culture in Āndhradēśa*, held on 17th-18th May, 2000, Hyderabad.
11. *E.I.,* XXIII, p. 70.
12. *Epigraphia Carnataka*, VII, S.K. 170.
13. S.I.I, IX, pt. II, *Bombay and Karnataka inscriptions*, XI, pt. II, No. 144.
14. Debala Mitra, *Op.cit.,* 1971, p. 193.
15. S. Aiyyappan and P.R. Srinivasan, *Story of Buddhism with special reference to South India*, Madras, 1960, p. 83.
16. *Ibid.*, 1960, p. 83.
17. Hara Prasad Sastri (Ed.) *Advaya Vajra Saṅgraha*, GOS, No. XL, Baroda, 1927, p. 41.
18. A. Aiyyappan and P.R. Srinivasan, *Op.cit.,* 1960, p. 85.
19. B. Bhattacharya, *The Indian Buddhist Iconography,* Calcutta, 1968, p. 49.
20. *Ibid.*, pp. 49-50.
21. B. Bhattacharya, *Op.cit.,* 1968, fig. 107.
22. *Ibid*, fig. 105.

23. *Ibid.*, fig.106.
24. Debala Mitra, *Op.cit.*, 1971, p. 109.
25. A. Aiyyappan and P.R. Srinivasan, *Op.cit.*, 1960, pp. 86-92.
26. *Annual report on South Indian Epigraphy*, 1920-21, part I, p. 8.
27. B. Bhattacharya, *Sādhanamāla,* GOS, No. 26 and 41, Oriental Institute, Baroda, 1925-28, pp. 65-66.
28. Alice Getty, *The Gods of Northern Buddhism*, Delhi, 1978, p. 69.
29. F.H. Gravely and T.N. Ramachandran, *Catalogue of Hindu Metal Images in the Madras Musem*, Madras, p. 108.
30. B. Bhattacharya, *Op.cit.*, 1968, p. 132, fig. 107.
31. S. Settar, 'A Buddhist *vihāra* at Aihole' *East and West, New Series,* Vol. 19, Nos. 1-2, March-June, 1969, pp. 126-138.
32. H. Cousens, *Chalukyan Architecture of the Canarese districts,* Calcutta, 1926, pp. 31-32.
33. P.B. Desai, *Op.cit.*, 1954, p. 85.
34. Srinivas Ritti, *Op. cit.*, 1989, p. 318.
35. *JESI,* Vol. II, pp. 67-68.
36. I.K. Sarma, *Studies in Early Buddhist monuments and Brahmi inscriptions of Andhra Pradesh,* Nagpur, 1958, p. 82.
37. Annual Report of the Mysore Archaeological Department for the year 1941, p. 84.
38. *Epigraphia Carnatika,* Vol. II, Shikarpur, No. 170.
39. *Ibid.*, No. 169.
40. K.Krishna Murthy, *Sculptures of Vajrayana Buddhism,* 1989, Delhi, p. 46.
41. *ARASI,* 1919-20, p. 38.
42. T.N. Ramachandran, *The Nagapaṭṭanam and other Bronzes in Madras Museum,* Vol. II, No. 1, Madras, 1950, p. 14.

# KERALA

The important Buddhist rulers of Kerala or Chēradēśa were the king Jayasiṁha Perumal who ruled the region of Quilon in Travancore in Ist c.B.C. and the other monarch was the king Bana Perumal (Baudha Perumal) in 3rd c.A.D. The great ruler of the Chēradēśa during medieval period was the king Vikramāditya Varugunan (9th c. A.D.) who ruled the territory with its capital Śrīmulavasam (Alwaye).[1] He was instrumental not only in propagating Buddhism in his kingdom but also to other regions of the Sub-continent. It was clearly confirmed by the discovery of an inscribed bronze image at Kandhar by Foucher. The label inscription on it reads '*Dakṣiṇapatte Mūlavamsa Lōkanāthe*' it means the ruler of Śrīmulavasam (of Chēradēśa).[2]

The evidences to support the existence of Buddhism in the region of Kerala are quite meagre except for the occurrence of a lone epigraphical reference in the Paliyam plates (868 A.D.) of Varaguna of the Vrishṇikula[3], wherein was found an invocation of Sauddhodani (Buddha), *Dharma* and *Saṅgha a*nd the discovery of a few images of Buddha at Karumadi, Bharanikkam, Marudukulangarai, Pallikkal and Mavelikkara.[4] Other evidences such as habitation sites and structural remains are yet to be reported. Of the five images so far reported two are taken up for the study and the remaining images though mutilated, found more developed than that of the Karumadi figure. On stylistic grounds, they are dated to 9th century A.D.

## MARUDUKULANGARAI

This village is in Karunagappali taluk of the former Travancore State and is very nearer to the city Trivendrum. The image discovered at the site is locally known as Marudukulangarai Buddha.[5] He is shown seated in *dhyāna mudrā* on a lotus pedestal. On iconographical features such as *uṣṇīṣa,* posture and facial expression, the image is dated to the post Gupta period (7th c.A.D). It is comparable with the sculptures reported from Kanchipuram particularly in delineation of the iconographical features.[6]

## KARUMADI

A mutilitated image of Buddha (3 ft. high) made of black basalt familiarly known as Karumadi Buddha was reported by the side of a canal located to the west of the Kamapuram temple near Karumadi.[7] Buddha (Amitābha) is seated in *dhyāna mudrā* on a pedestal with prominent *uṣṇīṣa* which represents like a flame of fire. The general tenor of workmanship is more developed than the Marudukulangarai sculpture. The well formed arms, the excellently modelled torso, smiling face may help to date the sculpture to the late Pallava times i.e. 7th-8th c.A.D. Images of this type having prominent flaming *uṣṇīṣa* were reported from Nagapaṭṭanam.[8] A *dhyāna* for his worship is mentioned in the *pañchakāra* section of the *Advayavajra Saṅgraha*.[9]

The images from this region can be compared with the figures of Anuradhapura in Ceylon, particularly in the depiction of drapery, *uṣṇīṣa*, posture and facial expression.[10] Thus the discovery of Buddha images in this corner of India obviously suggests that, the religion existed here at least from 1st c. B.C. to 9th c. A.D. i.e. the post Pallava times.

## REFERENCES

1. V.G. Nair, *Heritage of Buddhism (*Buddhism in South India), New Delhi, 1958, pp. 511-12.
2. D.C. Ahir, *Buddhism in South India,* New Delhi, 1992, p. 98.
3. T.A. Gopinatha Rao, 'Paliyam plates of Varuguna of Vrishnikula', Travancore Archaeological Series-I, 1910-13, p. 187 and Travancore Archaeological Series-II, Part-II, p. 116.
4. Debala Mitra, *Buddhist Monuments,* Calcutta, 1971, p. 192.
5. A. Aiyyappan and P.R. Srinivasan, *Story of Buddhism* (with special reference to South India), Madras, 1960, pp. 72-73.
6. Debala Mitra, *Op.cit.,* 1971, p. 194.
7. A. Aiyyappan and P.R. Srinivasan, *Op.cit.*, pp. 73-74.
8. Vidya Dehejia, 'The persistence of Buddhism in Tamil Nadu' *Marg,* XXXIX, p. 65.
9. Haraprasad Sastri, (ed.) *Advaya Vajra-Advaya Saṅgraha,* GOS, No. XL, Baroda, 1927, p. 41.
10. A. Aiyyappan and P.R. Srinivasan, *Op.cit.,* 1960, p. 73.

# CONCLUSION

The foregoing study helps us not only to understand the gradual transformation of a few Thēravāda or Mahāyāna Buddhist sites (such as Dhānyakaṭaka, Guntupalli and Salihundam etc. in Andhra Pradesh; Kanchipuram, Kaveripaṭṭanam and Nagapattanam in Tamilnadu, and Kadri and Belagami in Karnataka) into Vajrayāna centres, but also the origin and rise of *Pañcavīra* cult or *Pañcha* Buddha concept in South India. Though the doctrine of Mahāyāna witnessed a glorious epoch under the Sātavāhana, Ikṣvāku, Viṣṇukuṇḍi, Kadaṁba and Pallava rule (1st centuries A.D.-6th centuries A.D.), it was the Vajrayāna doctrine (4th centuries A.D.-5th centuries A.D.) that reinforced the slowly declining Buddhism and contributed for its continuity for a longer duration i.e. upto the post-Vijayanagara times (16th centuries A.D.) in South India.

The Buddhists who were on the verge of disappearing during 4th-5th centuries A.D., have shown tremendous leanings for Tāṅtricism with a view to obtain supernatural powers by which they could arrest the process of decline. This might have prompted the Vajrayāna Taṅtricists to innovate and introduce several Gods and Goddesses into the pantheon which ultimately gave rise to the emergence of God-cult and also the introduction of *Dhāraṇis*, *Maṇḍalas* and *Mudrās* alongwith Buddhist priest, *Vajrāchārya*.

Vajrayāna, considered to be the last phase of Buddhism in South India, is mainly represented by *Dhāraṇis* and *Maṅtras* as depicted on stone, clay tablets and a pantheon of Gods and Goddesses. The images and icons are very simple and small in size and constitute the earliest examples of Tāṅtric Buddhism. Comparatively, the North-Indian images are bigger in size and found to be chronologically later than the forms reported from South India. The heavily ornamented images, in some cases are shown as riding or trampelling the Hindu deities, which probably indicate not only the aversion of Vajrayāna Buddhists towards the Brāhmanical pantheon but also their spiritual supremacy over the Brāhmanical Gods and Goddesses. The images of Vajrayāna Buddhism in South India are generally simple, bereft of ornamentation, yet not exhibiting signs of depravity. The simplicity in carving the sculptures obviously suggests the absence of royal patronage and also the beginnings of God-cult in this region, whereas, the north Indian images are comparatively more ornamented, suggesting the economic and political support lent by the kings during the period.

In the beginning, the Theravādins or the early Buddhists worshipped Buddha symbolically in various forms such as *stūpa*, *swastika*, *Buddhapāda* depicted with *ashṭamaṅgala* symbols, *Dharmachakra*, Bōdhi tree, Throne, Pillar of fire etc. In course of time, the Mahāyanists considered the Buddha as Supreme God (Ādi-Buddha) and elevated Him to the position of a *Bhagavan* or *Lōkōttārā* and Buddha images were introduced for worship bearing some distinct features such as white colour, two broad and long eyes, prominent nose, a pair of long arms, beautiful chest, slightly fatty limbs and a prominent *uṣṇīṣa*. Thus, transformation of Buddhism from the state of aniconism to Mahāyāna or qualified theism was evident.

Subsequently, with the introduction of *Yōgacāra* school of philosophy, around 4th-5th centuries A.D. by *Yōgacārins* into orthodox Buddhism, a notable change was observed in the Buddhist ideology i.e. Buddhism became theistic. According to this school of pholosophy, the Taṅtricists considered Buddha as the supreme *Yōgi* or emperor among the *Yōgis* and began to conceive yōgic powers (*Yōga Śakti*) called *Kuṇḍalini* of Buddha, through which the spiritual power was generated from the base of the vertibral column up to the head, from which it bursts forth as divine flame (flaming *uṣṇīṣa*). This *Yōgacāra* concept spreads like wild fire not only by means of rituals but also by depicting the Buddha with flaming *uṣṇīṣa*.

The Taṅtricits or Vajrayānists who were the founders and followers of the new doctrine, introduced certain tenets and dogmas based on the principles of the *Śakta* and Śaiva sects to withstand the growing ideological concepts of the Brahmins. It was clearly noticed in the later forms of Mahāyānism, whose rituals and practices were almost identical with those of Saivism and Śaktism. As a result, divergence appeared in the case of individual icons indicating not only the existence of a number of sub-schools of the same form of religion, but also the freedom enjoyed by the sculptor in employing his dexterity to create new and newer forms. This may have been the main reason for the appearance of numerous forms of Gods and Goddesses in Vajrayāna Buddhism.

In Vajrayāna Buddhism, Buddha and his emanations are shown with unpleasant facial features and bodily forms which affected the super-human character. The serene and benign qualities of the earlier forms (Buddha in *Varada Mudrā* or

*Dhyāna Mudrā*), were substantially lowered by the plasticity of different bodily forms. The squarish nature of shoulders, unshapely and unpleasant body parts of the images, damaged the noble bodily features of Buddha. The ferocious expression of the face with eyes open and different postures suggest a feeling of horror rather than tranquility and devotion.

The period of 5th-6th centuries A.D. is considered to be an important hall-mark in the history of South India, particularly in religious context. This period witnessed the decline of Buddhism on the one hand and the revival of Vedic Brāhmanism, i.e. emergence of Hari-Hara cult, elevating *Śakti,* the supreme goddess on the other. During this period, the Buddhists lost their faith in their own exertions and needed the help of some God for easy salvation. More or less, similar tendency prevailed among the various sects of Brāhmanical faiths also. Therefore, naturally, the Tāṅtricists of both Brāhmanical and Buddhist faiths were forced to formulate several new tenets giving importance to *Śakti* in order to propagate and attract masses towards their religions. This resulted in the emergence of the concept of *Pañcavīra* cult by both the religions.

Under the religious banner of *Pañcavīra* cult, the Vajrayāna Buddhists invented the concept of *Pañca* Buddhas i.e. the five *Dhyāni* Buddhas, keeping Vairōcana as the central figure and the remaining four Buddhas *viz.* Ratnasaṁbhava, Amōghasiddhi, Amitābha and Akṣobhya on the four cardinal points, with a view to popularising the religion and also to withstand the strong influence of Brāhmanical tenets. The followers of the Brāhmanical faith, on the other hand, developed the concept of *Pañcavīra* cult, by combining the Brāhmanical tenets of *Śaiva* and *Vaiṣṇava* sects, keeping *Śakti* (Lajjagauri or Nude squatting mother goddess) as the central figure, flanked by Brahma and Narasimha on one side and Śiva and Skaṅda or Kārtikeya on the other in order to check the growing popularity of Buddhism.

The discovery of an inscribed pot sherd reading *Pañca*(*vīra*) dated to 4th-5th c.A.D. from Salihundam—a Buddhist site in north coastal Āndhradēśa coupled with *Pañcavīra* lime stone plaques from the early historic sites such as Addanki, Konedena, Darsi, Sarpavaram and Gopalapatnam datable to 5th-6th c. A.D. clearly attest to the existence of *Pañcavīra* cult in Āndhradēśa quite early.

Though Vajrayāna Buddhist literature speaks of *Śakti* as the embodiment of *karuṇa*, she never figures or occurs in the sculptured panels along with five *Dhyāni* Buddhas. Instead, five *Śaktis* or spouses were provided to the five *Dhyāni* Buddhas (namely Vajradhatvīśvari for Vairōcana, Lōchana for Akṣobhya, Mamaki for Ratna

Saṁbhava, Paṇḍāra for Amitābha and Tārā for Amōghasiddhi). These *Dhyāni* Buddhas are sculptured or portrayed with their *Śaktis* or spouses only in *yab-yum* (*yuganaddha)* posture symbolising the union of *Prajñā,* a feminine divinity with *karuṇa* (male). On the other hand, the Vajrayānists favoured a separate entity for *Śakti* in worship.

Recent surveys particularly in Āndhradēśa yielded several *Śakti* or Mother Goddess plaques (*Lajjāgauri* images) both in terracotta and in lime stone from several Buddhist sites such as Yeleswaram, Zuzur, Gopalapatnam, Karlapalem, Nagarjunakonda etc. Interestingly, the lime stone image from Nagarjunakonda bears an inscription (3rd centuries A.D.) in Brāhmi label characters reading "*Siddhaṁ Mahā dēviya avidhavaya Jivaputaya Mahārāja Siri Ehāvala Chāmtamūla-patiya khamduvulaya karintati* (*Karita iti*)". It says that 'the image (*Lajjāgauri* or Nude mother goddess) was caused to be made by Mahādevi Khamduvula, whose husband and son were alive and who was the wife of Mahārāja Siri Ehavala Chāmtamūla.' The above epigraphical evidence clearly speaks of the Goddess as the protector. Probably the same Goddess (*Lajjāgauri*) became Harītī (Śakti) in the later phase of Buddhism.

The origin of *Śakti* cult or mother Goddess (*Lajjāgauri*-fertility cult) can be traced to the Indus valley civilization of the Proto historic period and continued upto the Chālukya times (6th-7th centuries A.D.). Probably in the early historic times (1st-2nd centuries A.D.) the Buddhists might have borrowed the *Śakti* cult from one of the popularised and prevailing cults of ancient India and introduced it into their pantheon and gave her a separate entity.

After the 3rd centuries A.D., images of nude mother Goddess are conspicuously absent in Buddhist sites. In all probability the Goddess was conceived in the later phase of Buddhism as Harītī, attributed with all iconographical features whereas in the Brāhmanical pantheon she continued to appear as mother Goddess (*Lajjāgauri*) upto 6th-8th centuries A.D. The Goddess appeared in the form of *Śakti* or Parvati right from 2nd centuries A.D. onwards. Interestingly, the Chālukyas of Bādāmi in their epigraphs styled themselves as *Harītīputras*. Obviously, there is no such Goddess bearing the name Harītī in Brāhmanical pantheon and moreover so far no image of Harītī of Buddhist pantheon has been reported assignable to Chālukya sites. Thus epigraphical evidence leads us to believe that mother Goddess (*Lajjāgauri*) otherwise known as Harītī might be the *Kula-Dēvatā* or tutelary Goddess of the Bādāmi Chālukyas. This is also corroborated by the discovery of several images of the mother Goddess (*Lajjāgauri*) from the Chālukya sites in Krișṇa-Tuṅgabhadra valley.

Several lime stone plaques of *Lajjāgauri* (Mother Goddess) were also reported from Brāhmanical sites such as Konidena, Darsi, Addanki, depicting *Śakti* (*Lajjāgauri*) as the central figure flanked by Saivite and Vaishnavite Gods and images of larger size from Saivite temples like Vellala, Alampur, Keesaragutta, Pratakota, Miapuram, Sangamesvaram (datable to 6th-8th centuries A.D.) which suggests the status or importance given to the deity by the followers of Brāhmanical faith. She is also considered as the bestower or protector of children by them.

The above study clearly indicates that the Buddhists first introduced the worship of *Lajjāgauri* probably as *Śakti* in their pantheon and later on the others borrowed the cult and worshipped her in various forms along with other deities. Similarly the worship of Gaṇēśa. An early representation of the deity, Ganesa is noticed on the coping stone of a railimg at Amaravati. Mañjuśrī is also shown in the company of Viṣṇu and Gaṇēśa. Thus the Buddhist Gods also enjoy prominence in the Brāhmanical pantheon. Another goddess *viz.* Ugratārā or Tārā of Buddhists has also been incorporated by the Hindus. Thus, the Brāhmanical cult borrowed several deities from the Buddhist pantheon and later on frequent exchanges took place between the two religions depending up on the needs to meet religious exigency.

In Vajrayāna Buddhism, the concept of *Pañcavīra* cult or the five *Dhyāni* Buddhas and their emanations served as personified symbols of one or the other aspects of the Buddha and the doctrine. In this doctrine, the adept or Siddha conceptualises, literally enclosing them within their *maṇḍalas*, cosmic and magic diagrams and identifies himself with them in his meditational techniques. It appears that like the Mahāyāna system which made the attainment of Buddhahood easy as against the conservative school i.e. Thēravāda, similarly the Vajrayāna school of philosophy also reduces the lengthy and difficult process of attaining spiritual realisation and instant enlightenment.

Though Vajrayāna appeared outwardly as demoralised philosophy going against all the teachings of Buddha and the great patriarchs of the religion, it became very popular since its inception because of its cosmopolitan character.

Thus, the Vajrayāna is became mainly responsible for the introduction of God-cult and its worship and also for the advent of Buddhist priest, *Vajrāchārya*. Unfortunately this new ideological concept narrowed down the differences between Buddhism and Brāhmanism. As a result, the people at large were attracted more towards Brāhmanical tenets and dogmos. Added to this, the intellectual Brāhmins who tried to entrench Buddhism gradually turned away from Buddhism to the newly emerging concepts of Vedic-Brāhmanism, deserting the Buddhist *Saṅgha* which ultimately led to the gradual disappearance of Buddhism. Yet, sites like Dhānyakataka, Salihundam, Guntupalli, Mukhaliṅgam, Gummadidurru, Śaṅkaram in Andhra Pradesh; Nagapaṭṭanam, Kaveripaṭṭanam and Kanchipuram in Tamilnadu; Belgam and Kadri in Karnataka etc. survived upto the medieval and late medieval times as prosperous Vajrayāna Buddhist Centres in South India.

# BIBLIOGRAPHY


| | |
|---|---|
| Agrawala, V.S., | *Indian Art,* Varanasi, 1964. |
| Ahir, D.C., | *Buddhism in South India,* Delhi, 1992. |
| Aiyyappan, A., & Śrīvinasan, P.R., | *Story of Buddhism with Special Reference to South India,* Madras, 1960. |
| Bapat, P.V. (ed.) | *2500 years of Buddhism,* Delhi, 1987. |
| Barrett, Dauglas, | *Sculptures from Amaravati in the British Museum,* London, 1954. |
| Beal, S., | *Buddhist records of Western World,* translated from the Chinese of Hieun Tsang, London, 1906. |
| Bennet, A.A.G., | "Sukhavati literature", *Sambhasha-Mahā Bodhi Centenary commemorative volume,* Vol. I, No. 2, 1991. |
| Bhattacharya, B., (ed.) | *Sādhanamāla,* GOS, 2 Vols., Baroda, 1928. |
| | *Abhayakara Gupta's Niṣpanna Yōgavali,* GOS, No. CIX, Baroda, 1949, |
| | *The Indian Buddhist Iconography,* Calcutta, 1968. |
| Bhattasali, N.K., | *Iconography of Buddhist and Brāhmanical Sculptures in the Dacca Museum,* Delhi, 1972. |
| Chatterjee, H., | "An introduction to Yōgacāra School", *Sambhasha-Mahā Bodhi Centenary commemorative volume,* Vol. I, No. 2, 1991. |
| Christmas, H., | *Buddhism,* Great Britain, 1954. |
| Clark, W.E., | *Two Lamastic Pantheons,* 2 Vols., Cambridge, 1937. |
| Cousens, H., | *Chalukyan Architecture of the Canarese districts,* Calcutta, 1926. |
| Coomara Swamy, A.K., | *Elements of Buddhist Iconography,* Cambridge, 1935. |

Dasgupta, S.B. *An introduction to Tāntric Buddhism,* Calcutta, 1950.

Debala Mitra, *Buddhist Monuments,* Calcutta, 1971.

Desai, P.B., 'Buddhist Antiquities in Karanataka' *Journal of Indian History,* Vol. 32, 1954, p. 85.

"*A new Buddhist centre, JKU,* Vol. IV, Mysore, 1968.

Dhammaratana, H., *Buddhism in South India,* Ceylon, 1968.

Dutt, S., *Buddhist Monks and Monasteries in India,* New Delhi, 1960.

Gangooly, O.C., *Andhra Sculpture,* Hyderabad, 1973.

Getty, A., *The Gods of Northern Buddhism,* Delhi, 1978.

Gopinatha Rao, T.A., "Buddha Vestiges in Kanchipura', *I.A.*, New Delhi, 1915.

"Paliyam plates of Varuguna of Vrishnikula" *Travancore Archaeology Series I.*, Travancore, 1910-13.

Gordon, *Iconography of Tibetan Lamaism,* New York, 1939.

Gravely, F.H., & Ramachandran, T.N., *Catalogue of Hindu Metal images in Madras Museum,* Madras.

Gupte, R.S., *Iconography of the Hindus, Buddhists, Jains,* Bombay, 1973.

Hamid Kuraishi, Md., "Excavations at Alluru, Gummadidurru and Nagarjunakonda, *ARASI,* 1926-27.

Hanumantha Rao, D., "A unique sculpture of Gaṇapati from Sankaram" in I.K. Sarma and A.V.N. Murthy (eds.), *Śrī Rama Chandrika,* Delhi, 1993.

Hanumantha Rao, B.S.L., "Dhānyakaṭaka in Early Andhra History" *Andhradesa charitralo Dharaṇikōṭa,* Guntur, 1987.

*Buddhist Inscriptions of Āndhradēśa,* Hyderabad, 1998.

Hultzsch, H., 'A Pallava inscription at Amaravati', *South Indian inscriptions,* Vol. I, ASI, Delhi 1987.

Jayaswal, K.P., "Metal images of Kurkihar monastery, *JISOA, II,* No. 2, 1934.

Joshi, L.M., *Studies in Buddhist culture of India,* Delhi, 1967.

"Original Home of Tāṅtric Buddhism", *Journal of Oriental Institute,* Vol. XVI.

Krishna Murthy, K., *Mirrors of Indian Culture,* Delhi, 1982.

*Sculptures of Vajrayāna Buddhism,* Delhi, 1989.

Krishna Sastry, V.V., *Proto and Early Historic Cultures of Andhra Pradesh,* Hyderabad, 1983.

*Three grants of Pṛithvī Śrī Mūla Rāja from Kondavidu,* Hyderabad, 1992.

Longhurst, A.H., 'The Buddhist Monuments at Guntupalli, Krishna District', *ARASI,* Madras, 1916-17.

Marshall, John, 'Explorations at Ghantasala and Salihundam' *ARASI,* Calcutta, 1922.

Mani, V.R., *Sapta Mātṛikas in Indian Religion,* Delhi, 1995.

Michael Lockwood & Vishnu Bhatt. *Mattavilasa Prahāsana,* Madras, 1981.

Mitra, D., "Astamahabhaya Tārā" *JAS,* Vol. XXXII, No. 1, 1957,.

"Jambhala-Maṇḍalas in Sculpture" *JAS,* III, No. 1, 1961.

Nagaraju, S., Vestiges of Buddhist art (Heritage of Karnataka) Marg, Vol. XXXXV, No.1.

*Buddhist Architecture of Western India,* Delhi, 1986.

Peter Della Santina, *The Tree of Enlightenment,* Taiwan, 1997.

Raghavachary, K., "Dharaṇikōṭa and its western contacts' *QRHS,* XII, No. 3, Calcutta, 1972-73.

Rama, K., *Buddhist Art of Nagarjunakonda,* New Delhi, 1995.

Ramachandra Rao, P.R., *Andhra Sculpture,* Hyderabad, 1984.

Ramachandra, T., & Venkata Ramanayya, B. — *Lalitha Vistharam,* Hyderabad, 1969.

Ramachandran, K.S., — *Archaeology of South India,* Tamil Nadu, 1980.

Ramachandran, T.N., — "Nagarjunakonda", *MASI,* Calcutta, 1938.

*The Nagapattanam and other Buddhist Bronzes in the Madras Museum,* Madras, 1965.

Ramachandra Murthy, N.S., — "Excavations at Kotalingala, Karimnagar district", *AAR,* A&M, Hyderabad, 1981.

Rama Rao, M., — "Buddhism and Buddhist Monuments in A.P.", *Buddha Jayanti Souvenir,* Guntur, 1956.

Ramaswamy A., — *History of Pondicherry,* Delhi, 1987.

Ramesan, N., — *Copper plate inscriptions of Andhra Pradesh Government Museum*, 1902, p. 36, Pl. (1) a.

Rea A., — *South Indian Buddhist Antiquities,* Madras, 1894.

"Excavations at Amaravati", *ARASI,* Calcutta, 1905-06.

"Explorations and Excavations of ancient sites", *ARASI,* Calcutta, 1908-09.

Rhys Davids, T.W. (ed.) — *Thomas Watter's Hieun Tsang Travels in India,* Delhi, 1961.

Robert Sewell, — *List of Antiquarian Remains in Madras Presidency,* Vol. I, London, 1883.

Sama Srami, S., (ed.) — *Karnda Vyuha,* Calcutta, 1968.

Sarcar, D.C., — *Select Inscriptions,* Delhi, 1965.

Sarma, I.K., — "Unique Uṣṇīṣa (coping stone) from Amaravati", in *Śrī Mallampalli Somasekhara Sarma, commemoration volume,* Hyderabad, 1982.

"Some more inscriptions from Amaravati excavations and the chronology of the Mahāstūpa" *JESI,* 1974.

*Studies in Early Buddhist Monuments and Brahmi inscriptions of Āndhradēśa,* Nagapur, 1988.

"Archaeological evidences pertaining to Buddhism in Tamil Nadu" ed. I.K. Sarma and A.V.N. Murthy (ed.), *Ratna Chandrika,* Delhi, 1993.

Sastry, D.L.N., Excavations at Nelakondapalli, Khammam district (unpublished report), A & M, Hyderabad, 1999.

Sastri, H.P., *Advavaya Vajra Saṅgraha,* GOS No.XI, Baroda, 1927.

Sastry, T.V.G. (et al) *Vaddamanu Excavations,* Hyderabad, 1988.

Sathiantha Iyer, R., *Studies in Ancient History of Tondaimaṇḍalam,* Madras, 1944.

S. Settar "A Buddhist Vihara at Aihole, *East and West, New Series,* Vol. 19, Nos. 1-2, 1926, pp. 31-32.

Shetty, Vasantha, B., *Studies in Karnataka History,* Delhi, 1984.

Sir Aruel Stein., *Report of the Archaeological Society of India,* Frontier Circle, London, 1912.

Sivarama Murthy, C., *Amaravati Sculptures in the Madras Govt. Museum.,* Madras, 1942.

Srinivasan, L.K., "Some medieval sculptures from Ratnal district, Meerut" I.K. Sarma, A.V.N. Murty (eds.) *Śrī Ramachandrika,* New Delhi, 1993.

Srinivas Ritti, "Buddhism in Kannada inscriptions'', ed., Devendra Handa & Ashvini Agrawal, *Ratna Chandrika,* Delhi, 1989.

Subrahmanyam, B., "Excavations at Gopalapatnam", *AAR,* 1993-94, A & M, Hyderabad.

Subramanian, K.R., *Buddhist Remains in Andhra,* Madras, 1932.

Subramanyam, R., *Salihundam (*A Buddhist site in Andhra Pradesh*),* Hyderabad, 1964.

Tripathi, S., *Guhya Samaja Tantra (Tathāgata Guhyaka),* Sanskrit Series, No. 9, Darbanga, 1988.

Vaidyanathan, K.R., *Temples and legends of Kerala,* Bombay, 1982.

Venkata Ramanayya, N., *Inscriptions of Andhra Pradesh, Warangal district,* Hyderabad, 1974.

Vidya Dehejia, "The persistence of Buddhism in Tamil Nadu", *Marg,* Vol. XXXIX, No. 4.

Waddell, "Evolution of Buddhist cult, its Gods, images and Art" *IAQR,* 1912.

Yazdani, G., *Ajanta,* Part I-IV, London, 1930-33-46 and 55.

Zimmer, H., *The Art of Indian Asia*, 2 Vols., New York, 1955.

Zwalf, W., *Buddhism, Art and Faith,* London, 1985.

# INDEX


## A

Abhayakaragupta, 7.
Addanki, 103.
Advayavajra Saṅgraha, 3, 7, 49, 55, 59, 73, 74, 78, 89, 98
Aihole, 93.
Akṣobhya, 5, 17, 30, 31, 33, 34, 37, 38, 39, 42, 50, 51, 60, 75, 78, 101.
Alangudipatti, 71.
Alexander Rea, 19.
Alluru, 16.
Alupa, 91.
Amaravati, 11, 14, 16, 17, 23, 24, 27, 29, 39, 48, 50, 53, 55, 56, 60, 61, 62, 73, 78, 79, 80, 81, 92, 94, 95, 103.
Amitābha, 5, 17, 18, 33, 43, 44, 46, 47, 53, 55, 56, 59, 62, 73, 78, 79, 81, 82, 89, 91, 92, 93, 101, 101, 102.
Amitaya sūtra, 7.
Amōgha Siddhi, 5, 36, 48, 101, 102.
Anaṅga Vajra, 7.
Ānandagōtrins, 15.
Ananta Varma Chōḍa Gaṅga, 15, 42.
Anuradhapura, 98.
Aparājita, 25.
Aparamahā Vinasēliya, 26.
Āryadēva, 9.
Ārya Mārīcī, 45.
Asaṅga, 2, 7.
Aśōka, 12, 13, 42, 44, 70, 87, 88.
Aśōka Kāṇṭa, 45.
Assaka, 13.
Aṣṭasahaśrika Prajñā Pāramitā, 45.
Aśvaghōṣa, 4.
Avalōkitēśwara, 5, 6, 8, 17, 18, 29, 33, 35, 39, 40, 41, 46, 48, 61, 77, 78, 79, 92, 93, 94.

## B

Bahusrutīya, 26.
Bāllāladēva, 88.
Bāṇa Perumāl, 97.
Bāvari, 13.
Bayyamāṁba, 18.
Belagami, 94, 99, 104.
Bharaṇikkam, 97.
Bhadanta Nāgārjunāchārya, 9.
Bhadrapāla, 43.
Bhairava, 34.
Bhattiprolu, 11.
Bhāvavivēka, 9.
Bhīma, 12.
Bhūtapāla, 87.
Biṅdusāra, 13.
Bōdhisattva Vādana Kalpalatā, 20.
Brahmagiri, 12, 87.
Brahmānanda, 37.
Buddham, 16, 29, 53, 61, 62.
Buddhamitra, 9.

## C

Chālukya, 19, 21, 28, 88, 93, 94, 102.
Chandavaram, 16.
Chaṅdraprabha, 9.
Chēra, 97.
Chōla, 71, 77, 79, 81, 95.

## D

Darikapa, 7.
Darsi, 103.
Dasavala, 8.
Dhammachēti, 71, 76.

Dharaṇikōta, 7, 8, 12, 15, 16, 27, 28, 29, 56, 99, 104.
Dhānyakaṭaka, 7, 8, 12, 15, 16, 27, 28, 29, 56, 99, 104
Dhānyavāṭaka, 7, 8, 12, 15, 16, 27, 28, 29, 56, 99, 104
Dhānyaṁkapuram, 7, 8, 12, 15, 16, 27, 28, 29, 56, 99, 104
Dannalakōṭa, 7, 8, 12, 15, 16, 27, 28, 29, 56, 99, 104
Dhannāḍa 7, 8, 12, 15, 16, 27, 28, 29, 56, 99, 104
Dharaṇī Saṁgraha, 45, 49.
Dharmadhātu Vāgīśvara, 8, 17, 22, 24, 51.
Dharmmadēva, 54.
Dharmakīrti, 9, 15, 28.
Dharmakōśa Saṅgraha, 18.
Dharmapāla, 9, 36.
Dhulikatta, 21, 27.
Dhyānabhadra, 70.
Digñāga, 9.

E

Ehuvala Chaṁtamula, 87.
Elaiyur, 55, 59, 71, 73.

G

Gaganagrnñja, 90.
Gaṇapati, 22, 23.
Gautama, 5, 31.
Gautamīputra Sātakarṇi, 25.
Gautamīputra Vijaya Sātakarṇi, 25.
Gavimath, 87.
Ghantasala, 16.
Gōbhada, 13, 14.
Goli, 53, 60.
Gopalapatnam, 16.
Guhya, 7.
Guhya Siddhi, 7.
Gummadidurru, 12, 15, 16, 29, 50, 53, 54, 79, 104.
Guṇakāraṇḍa Vyūha, 18.
Guntupalli, 12, 16, 49, 52, 94, 99, 104.

H

Harītī, 19, 20, 21, 22, 26, 27, 58.
Hayagrīva, 89.
Heruka, 16, 17, 29, 33, 34, 35.
Hēvajra, 34, 35.
Hieun Tsang, 8, 9, 18, 28, 33, 75.
Hīnayāna, 4, 12, 31, 32.

I

Ikṣvāku, 14, 15, 87, 97.
Iṅdhrabhūti, 7.
Itsing, 21, 76

J

Jaggayyapeta, 8.
Jalandharipa, 7.
Jambhala, 38, 39, 81.
Jaya Prabha, 9.
Jñāna Siddhi, 7.
Jayanakonda Cholapuram, 71, 74, 82.
Jayasiṁha Perumal, 97.

K

Kadamba, 88, 99.
Kadri, 12, 99, 104.
Kālarātri, 34.
Kaliṅga, 12, 13.
Kamākhya, 7.
Kaṁvayasiri, 13, 14.
Kanakamuni, 5.
Kanchipuram, 12, 70, 71, 74, 75, 78, 82, 97, 99, 104.
Kandhar, 48, 53, 94, 97.
Kanaganahalli, 12, 88.
Kanikilippai, 71.
Kanuparthy, 12.

Karumadi, 97.
Karur, 71.
Kāśyapa, 5.
Kaveripattanam, 12, 70, 71, 79, 104.
Kēshavadēva, 94.
Kēta II, 28.
Khadiravāṇi Tārā, 35, 81.
Khagarbha, 90.
Khailkair, 48, 53.
Khasarpana, 48, 53.
Khasarpana Lōkanātha, 46, 47, 48.
Kolivada, 94.
Kollapattu, 55, 59, 73, 83.
Kondapur, 12.
Konedena, 103.
Kōsala, 13.
Kōṭa, 15.
Kotalingala, 12, 14.
Krakuchanda, 5.
Krishṇanaṅda, 37.
Kriyāsamuccaya, 7.
Kṣēmēndra, 20.
Kṣitigarbha, 90.
Kuan-yin, 18.
Kuberaka, 11.
Kui-tzu-mushen, 21.
Kumaragupta, 7.
Kumariasammaliya 11.
Kunḍala, 19.
Kundavarma, 92.
Kunthuru, 55, 59, 83.
Kurkihar, 72, 75.
Kuvam, 71, 82.

L

Lajjagauri, 22, 27, 101, 102, 103.
Lalita Vistāra, 13.
Lōkanātha, 88, 89, 90, 91.
Lōchana, 101.
Lōkēśvara, 29, 35, 41, 81, 88, 89, 91, 92, 93, 95.
Luipha, 7.

M

Madagaram, 73.
Mādharīputra Vīrapurushadatta, 25.
Mādhyamika Vāda, 2, 3.
Mahācina Tāra, 35, 36, 37.
Mahākātyāyana, 13.
Mahāmayūrī, 50.
Mahāraṭhis, 87.
Mahāvastu, 21, 58.
Mahāvidya, 80.
Mahāyāna, 1, 3, 4, 12, 14, 15, 22, 29, 32, 52, 93, 95, 101, 104 .
Mahēṅdravarman, 15, 70.
Mahisāsaka, 26.
Maitrēya, 5, 29, 31, 33, 39, 50, 72, 79, 80, 90.
Mamaki, 101.
Manambady, 73.
Mangalore, 89.
Manganallur, 71.
Manikandi, 71, 82.
Maṇimēkalai, 18, 70, 74.
Maṇidhara, 80.
Mañjughōsha, 41, 42, 51, 52, 88.
Mañjuśrī, 5, 29, 41, 42, 46, 51, 52, 103.
Mañjuśrī Mūlataṅtra, 7, 28, 51.
Mañjuvajra, 51.
Maṅtrayāna, 1, 2, 3, 4, 12, 14, 15, 22, 29, 32, 52, 81, 89, 93, 95, 99, 100.
Marcopolo, 76.
Marīcī, 42, 43, 45, 46, 50.
Marudukulangarai, 97.
Maski, 12, 87.
Mattavilāsa Prahasana, 15.
Mauggalayana, 54.
Mavelikkara, 97.
Melaiyur, 33, 71, 72, 77.
Mukhalingam, 56, 104.
Mulaka, 12.

N

Nagapattanam, 12, 55, 70, 71, 77, 89, 95, 98, 104.

Nāgārjuna, 1, 7, 8, 25, 26.
Nagarjunakonda, 7, 9, 16, 25, 26, 53, 55, 58, 87.
Nāgavādana, 76.
Nāgiyaka, 94,.
Nalanda, 72.
Nanadalur, 16.
Nandayapalem, 53.
Nārana, 13, 14.
Narasimha Varman-II, 71.
Naropā, 7.
Nelakondapalli, 16, 29, 53, 61, 80.
Niṣpannayōgāvali, 7, 23, 24, 31, 32, 33, 35, 45, 52, 71, 78.

P

Padmapāṇi, 29, 33, 39, 40, 50, 53, 54, 60, 61, 62, 80.
Padmavajra, 7.
Palkigundu, 87.
Pallava, 40, 71, 72, 81, 98, 99.
Pallavanēśwaram, 71.
Pallikkal, 97.
Pallīśvaram, 71.
Pallur, 71.
Paṇḍāra, 102.
Panduka, 20.
Parṇaśabari, 25.
Patna, 31.
Pavuralakonda, 16.
Penumaka, 16.
Perunjeru, 71.
Piṅgala/Pilingika, 20.
Pliny, 13.
Pondicherry, 82.
Potalaka, 8, 18, 47.
Prajñāpāramita Saṁgraha, 9.
Prithivīśrī Mūlarāja,
Ptolemy, 76.
Pugalur, 71.
Pugama, 71.
Purnagiri, 7.

R

Rāhu, 44.
Rāhula, 54
Rajagriha, 13, 20.
Ramatirtham, 16, 17, 53, 56, 58, 79.
Rashṭrakūṭa, 72.
Ratnagiri, 79.
Ratnapāṇi, 5.
Ratnasaṁbhava, 5, 38, 57, 101.
Ravivarma, 88.

S

Ṣaḍakṣarī Lōkēśwara, 80.
Saddharma Ratnakāra, 28.
Sādhanamāla, 7, 17, 18, 23, 24, 29, 30, 32, 34, 36, 37, 38, 41, 44, 45, 47, 49, 51, 52, 57, 80.
Śākyamuni, 58.
Sālankāyana, 14, 15.
Salihundam, 8, 12, 15, 16, 31, 36, 42, 43, 53, 54, 56, 60, 62, 79, 80, 95, 99, 101, 104.
Samagōpa, 13, 14.
Sāmantabhadra, 5, 90.
Samyukta Vastu, 20.
Sankaram, 12, 16, 19, 22, 27, 31, 54, 104.
Sannati, 11, 12, 87, 88.
Sāntarakṣita, 7.
Saraha, 7.
Saranath, 31, 39, 91.
Sarvajñnamitra, 48.
Sātavāhana, 19, 54, 56, 59, 61, 87, 88.
Sathanmalli, 71.
Saundarānanda, 4.
Sēkōddēsaṭīka, 28.
Siddhārtha, 60.

Silappādikaram, 70.
Simhavarman, 9, 28.
Sirihatta, 7.
Śivamaka Vijaya, 59.
Śivaskandavarman, 15.
Śivaśrī Pulumāvi, 87.
Sōmaka, 11.
Śrī Mādhrīputra Vīrapurushadatta, 70.
Śrīmūlavasam, 97.
Srong Tsangampo, 8.
Suddhōdana, 3.
Sudhāna Kumāra, 42, 47.
Sugati Sandarsana Lōkēśvara, 35.
Sūnyavāda, 19.
Suttanipata, 13.
Suttapīṭaka, 35, 36.

T

Taipa, 7.
Takkallāpadu, 57, 58.
Tantrasāra, 37, 38.
Tantrayāna, 1, 2, 75.
Tārā, 18, 36, 37, 42, 44, 47.
  Ārya Tārā, 48.
  Sita Tārā, 49, 50, 57, 81, 88, 89, 90, 94, 102, 103.
  Tāriṇī Tārā, 49.
  Ugra Tārā, 49, 50, 57, 81, 88, 89, 90, 94, 102, 103.
  Vajra Tārā, 49, 50, 57, 81, 88, 89, 90, 94, 102, 103.
Tārānāth, 7, 18.
Tārārahasya, 37.
Tattva Ratnāvali, 3.
Tattva Saṅgraha, 7.
Theravāda, 4, 16, 103.
Thotlakonda, 15.
Tirumangai, 76.
Tiruvalanjuli, 71.
Tiruvvatti, 55, 71, 74.
Trailōkyakṣēpa, 35.
Trailōkyamalla, 94.
Tribhuvanamalladēva, 15.
Tyaganur, 71, 72.

U

Uddiyana, 7.

V

Vadali, 44.
Vaddamanu, 11.
Vaikunthapuram, 59.
Vairōcana, 5, 33, 44, 57, 101.
Vajrabōdhi, 9, 75.
Vajradhātvīśvari, 45, 101.
Vajrāṅkusi, 91.
Vajrachārya, 103.
Vajrapāṇi, 5, 29, 90.
Vajravatinamamaṇḍalōpāyika, 7.
Vajrayāna, 1, 3, 4, 6, 7, 9, 11, 12, 14, 15, 16, 24, 25, 26, 29, 52, 53, 54, 56, 62, 71, 75, 76, 88, 89, 95, 99, 100, 1-3, 104.
Vāgīśvara, 46.
Vaibhāṣika, 1.
Vaṁsadhāra, 12, 42.
Varāhomukhi, 44.
Varāli, 44.
Vāsishṭīputra Chāntamula, 25.
Vāsishṭīputra Ehavula Chāntamula, 25.
Vāsishṭīputra Pulumāvi, 25.
Vāsishṭīputra Rudra Purushadatta, 25.
Vasudhara, 81.
Vattali, 44.
Vellanore, 71.
Vellandallur, 71.
Velippalayam, 77.
Vijayapa, 7.
Vijayapuri, 25.

Vijayōttunga Varma, 71.
Vijayanagara, 77, 99.
Vighnāntaka, 25.
Vigñānavāda, 2.
Vikramāditya Varagunam, 97.
Vikrampur, 25.
Vimānavattu, 13.
Vinaya Pīṭaka, 20.
Vinhukada Chutukulānanda Sātakarṇi, 87.
Vīrapurushadatta, 25.
Viṣkambhim, 90.
Vishṇukuṇḍi, 14, 15, 61.
Viśvapāṇi, 5.

W

Walter Elliot, 71.

X

Xian Chun, 71.

Y

Yajña Śrī Sātakarṇi, 25.
Yamāntaka, 42.
Yōgacāra, 3, 100.
Yōgēśvari, 22.

Z

Zaingganaing, 71.
Zuzur, 102

✧✧✧

# PLATES

1. (c) Heruka, Gopalapatnam, Visakhapatnam District.

2. Avalōkiteśvara, Ramatirtham,
Prakasam Dist.

3. Inscribed clay tabalets with *Dhāranis,* Sankaram, Visakhapatnam Dist.

4. Buddha (Amitābha), Sankaram, Visakhapatnam Dist.

5. Harītī, Sankaram, Visakhapatnam Dist.

6. Bronze Icon of Harītī, Dhulikatta, Visakhapatnam Dist.

7. Harītī, Karkaipalle, Visakhapatnam Dist.

8. Tantric Image of Gaṇapati, Sankaram, Visakhapatnam Dist.

9. Harītī, Nagarjunakonda, Guntur Dist.

10. Bronze Icons of Buddha, Amaravati, Guntur Dist.

11. Bronze Icons of Avalōkiteśvara, Amaravati, Guntur Dist.

12. Buddha (Akṣobhya), Amaravati, Guntur Dist.

13. Maitrēya, Amaravati, Guntur Dist.

14. Buddha and Padmapāni, Amaravati, Guntur Dist.

15 (a) Heruka, Amaravati, Guntur Dist.

16. Sugati Sandarśanalōkēśvara, Amaravati, Guntur Dist.

17. Khadiravaṇī Tārā, Amaravati, Guntur Dist.

17. (a) Syāma Tārā, Amaravati, Guntur Dist.

18. Heruka, Ugra Tārā & Maitreya, Amaravati, Guntur Dist.

19. Jambhāla (stucco), Amaravati, Guntur Dist.

20. Buddha flanked by Maitrēya and Padmapāṇi, Amaravati, Guntur Dist.

21. Padmapāṇi, (British Museum, London), Amaravati, Guntur Dist.

21 (a) Padmapāṇi, (British Museum, London), Amaravati, Guntur Dist.

22. Avalōkiteśvara (British Museum, London), Amaravati, Guntur Dist.

23. Buddha (Akṣobhya) (Madras Museum), Amaravati, Guntur Dist.

24. Siṁhanāda Avalōkiteśvara, (Madras Museum), Amaravati, Guntur Dist.

25. Mañjughōsha (Madras Museum), Amaravati, Guntur Dist.

26. Buddha (Stucco), Salihundam, Srikakulam Dist.

27. Mārīcī, Salihundam, Srikakulam Dist.

27. (a) Back view (Mārīcī), Salihundam, Srikakulam Dist.

28. Mārīcī, Salihundam, Srikakulam Dist.

29. Vāgīśvara, Salihundam, Srikakulam Dist.

30. Khasarpaṇa, Salihundam, Srikakulam Dist.

31. Tārā, Salihundam, Srikakulam Dist.

32. Sita Tārā, Salihundam, Srikakulam Dist.

33. Maitreya, Salihundam, Srikakulam Dist.

34. Padmapāṇi, Salihundam, Srikakulam Dist.

35. Buddha (Akṣobhya), Salihundam, Srikakulam Dist.

36. Buddha (Akṣobhya), Salihundam, Srikakulam Dist.

37. Mañjusri, Salihundam, Srikakulam Dist.

38. Bronze Icon of Padmapāṇi, Guntupalli, West Godavari Dist.

39. Avalōkitēśvara, Gummadidurru, Krishna Dist.

40 Buddha (Amitābha), Kunthuru, Nellore Dist.

42. Buddha (Amitābha) Mukhalingam, Srikakulam Dist.

41. Buddha (Akṣobhya) Mukhalingam, Srikakulam Dist.

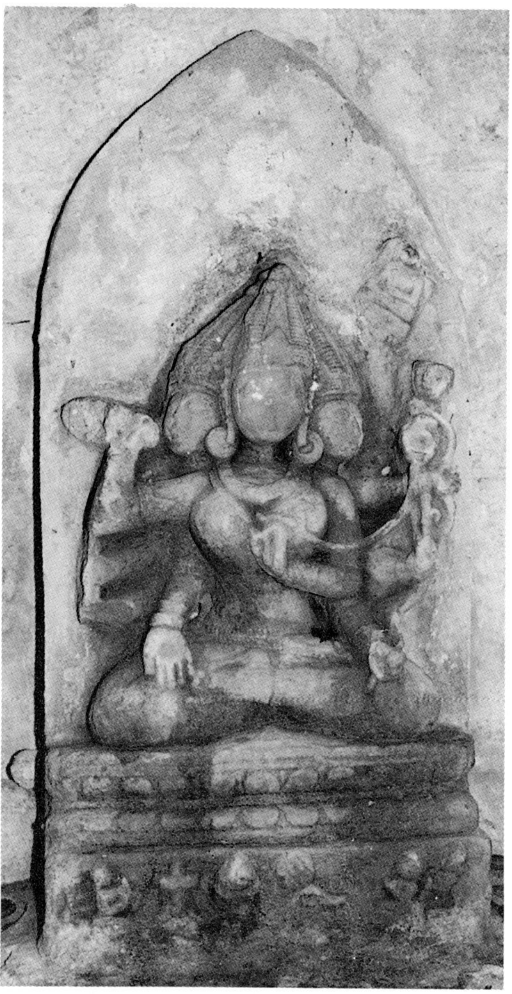

43. Uṣṇiṣa Vijaya, Mukhalingam, Srikakulam Dist.

44. Harītī, Takkallapadu, Krishna Dist.

45. Buddha (Amitābha), Kollapattu, Nellore Dist.

46. Buddha (Akṣobhya), Vaikunthapuram, Guntur Dist.

47. Padmapāni, Nandayapalem, Guntur Dist.

48. Bronze Icons of Buddha as Padmapāṇi, Buddham, Guntur Dist.

49. Bronze Icon of Avalōkitēśvara (Front and Back views), Nelakondapalli, Khammam Dist.

50 (a) Head of Avalōkitēśvara showing silver inlaid eyes and *uṛṇa,* Nelakonda-palli, Khammam Dist.

50 (b) Close up view of Avalōkitēśvara, Nelakondapalli, Khammam Dist.

51. Maitrēya, Melaiyur, Tanjore Dist.

52. Buddha in dhyāna mudrā, Tyagnur, Salem Dist.

52 (a) Buddha in dhyāna mudrā, Tyagnur, Salem Dist.

53. Buddha (Amitābha), Elaiyur, Tanjore Dist.

54. Buddha (Amitābha), Manambady, Tanjore Dist.

54 (a) Bronze icon of standing Buddha with flaming *uṣṇīṣa,* Tanjore, Tanjore Dist.

55. Buddha (Amitābha), Tanjore, Tanjore Dist.

56. Buddha (Amitābha), Tiruvatti, South Arcot Dist.

57 (b) Buddha (Amitābha), Jayanakonda Cholapuram, Tiruchirapalli Dist.

57 (a) Buddha (Amitābha), Jayanakonda Cholapuram, Tiruchirapalli Dist.

57 (c) Buddha (Amitābha), Jayanakonda Cholapuram, Tiruchirapalli Dist.

58. Buddha (Akṣobhya), Kanchi-puram.

59. Buddha (Amitābha), Kanchi-puram.

60 (a) Buddha, Kanchipuram.

60 (b) Buddha, Kanchipuram.

60 (c) Buddha, Kanchipuram.

61. Bronze Icon of Buddha with flaming *uṣṇīṣa,* Nagapattanam.

61 (a) Buddha (Akṣobhya), Nagapattanam.

62. Buddha in *vyakhyana mudrā (Bronze),* (Fine Arts Museum, Boston), Nagapattanam.

63. Buddha (Akṣobhya), Nagapattanam.

63 (a) Buddha in *dhyāna mudrā* (11th c. A.D., Norton Simon Museum of Arts, Pasadena), Nagapattanam.

63 (b) Head of a Buddha with flaming *uṣṇīṣa* (11th c. A.D.) (Art Institute of Chicago), Nagapattanam.

63 (c) Amitābha (9th c. A.D.) (The Brooklyn Museum), Nagapattanam.

64. Buddha (Amitābha) Bronze, Nagapattanam.

65. Avalōkitēśvara, Nagapattanam.

65 (a) Avalōkitēśvara (17th A.D.), Bronze, Nagapattanam.

66. Maitrēya (Bronze, Front & Back views), Nagapattanam.

67. Maitrēya (Bronze), Nagapattanam.

67 (a) Maitrēya (17th A.D. Bronze), Nagapattanam.

68. Ṣaḍakṣari Lōkēśvara (Bronze), Nagapattanam.

69. Padmapāṇi (Bronze), Nagapattanam.

70. Khadiravāṇi Tārā (Bronze), Nagapattanam.

70 (a) Tārā (Bronze), Nagapattanam.

71. Lōkēśvara (Bronze), Nagapattanam.

72. Jambhala (Bronze), Nagapattanam.

74. Buddha (Amitābha), Mani-kandi, Ramanathapuram Dist.

73. Jaṁbhala and Vasudhara, Nagapattanam.

75. Buddha (Amitābha), Kuvam, Chengalput Dist.

76. Buddha (Amitābha), Arikamedu, Pondicherry.

77. Buddha (Amitābha), Karadikuppam, Pondicherry.

78. Buddha in *vyakhyana mudrā* (Bronze), Kadri, Mangalore.

79. Lōkanātha (Bronze), Kadri, Mangalore.

80. Hālāhala Lōkēśvara (Bronze), Kadri, Mangalore.

81. Close up view, Hālāhala, showing inlaid silver eyes and *urṇa,* Kadri, Mangalore.

82. Tārā-Bhagavati, Belagami, Shimoga Dist.